## Photo credits

Unless otherwise noted, all skull images are the property of
Skulls Unlimited, LLC and are used by permission

Alligator – H. Zell/Wikimedia Commons, Baby alligator - Steve Hillebrand, U.S. Fish and Wildlife Service/Wikimedia Commons, Gray Wolf – Gary Kramer/U.S. Fish and Wildlife Service/Wikimedia Commons, Babirusa - Masteraah at de.wikipedia , Beaver – By Steve from Washington, DC, usa/Wikimedia Commons, Cottontail rabbit - Clinton & Charles Robertson from Del Rio, Texas & College Station, TX, USA/Wikimedia Commons, Zebra - Lilla Frerichs/Publicdomainpictures.net, Boxer dog – Vicki Mitchell/Wikimedia Commons, Egyptian fruit bat - Arpingstone/Wikimedia Commons, Bat-eared fox - Yathin S Krishnappa/Wikimedia Commons, King Mackerel - Brandi Noble-NOAA/NMFS/SEFSC/Wikimedia Commons, Piranha - Greg Hume/Wikimedia Commons, Striped hyena – Sumeet Moghe/Wikimedia Commons, Iguana – Šarūnas Burdulis/Wikimedia Commons, Western diamondback rattlesnake - H. Krisp/Wikimedia Commons, Rattlesnake rattles - Bubba73 (You talkin' to me?), (Jud McCranie) /Wikipedia Commons, Water monitor - Olexandr Topchylo/Wikimedia Commons, Mandrill – Cburnett/Wikimedia Commons, Bald eagle - Adrian Pingstone (Arpingstone)/Wikimedia **Commons**, Chimpanzee - Thomas Lersch/Wikimedia Commons, Llama – Jean-Pol GRANDMONT/Wikimedia Commons, Rhinoceros – Randall Lee/ PublicDomainPictures.net, Kangaroo - "Red kangaroo - melbourne zoo"/Wikimedia Commons, Kangaroo - "- fighting red kangaroos 1" by Dellex - Own work/Wikimedia Commons, Aye-aye - Frank Vassen/Wikimedia Commons, African lion – Kevin Pluck/Wikimedia Commons, Sheep – Karen Arnold/Publicdomainpictures.net, Gorilla – Harvey Barrison/Wikimedia Commons, White-tailed deer - Clay Heaton/Wikimedia Commons, Great Seal of the United States - U.S. Government/ Wikimedia Commons, Racoon - Judy Weggelaar/Wikimedia Commons, Water monitor – Antony Stanley from Gloucester, UK/ Wikimedia Commons, Shoebill - Hjalmar Gislason from Reykjavik, Iceland /Wikimedia Commons, Shoebill - "Gőtehal-2" by Gőtehal.jpg: Mathaederivative work: Bff - Gőtehal.jpg/WikiMedia Commons, Hippopotamus - "Hippopotamus - 04" by Kabacchi - Hippopotamus - 04/Wikimedia Commons, Hippo mouth opening" by Jon Connell - Yawning hippo/Wikimedia Commons, Gorilla – Mark Dumont (Contemplation  Uploaded by Snowmanradio)/Wikimedia Commons, King Kong poster - "Kingkongposter" by Keye Luke - www.widescreenmuseum.com, Piranha by Karelj (Own work) via Wikimedia Commons, Piranha jaw - Jaw of the piranha by Andrewself (talk)/Wikipedia.org, "TaleofPeterRabbit8" by Beatrix Potter/Wikisource ebook of The Tale of Peter Rabbit. Via Wikipedia, "Down the Rabbit Hole" by John Tenniel - optimization of Image:De Alice's Abenteuer im Wunderland Carroll pic 02.jpg./Wikimedia Commons, "Llama lying down" by Johann "nojhan" Dréo - IMG_1418/Wikimedia Commons, "Llama with numbers" by Manco Capac - Own work/en.wikipedia.org, Huey Long - "HueyPLongGesture" by Uncredited news photographer. - United States Library of Congress's Prints and Photographs division/Wikipedia.org,

**Answers to Skulls match (left to right):**
Top row: Beaver, Gorilla, Tiger
Second row: Hippopotamus, Rabbit, Llama
Third row: Water monitor, Aye-Aye, Babirusa

# SKULLS

Copyright © 2015 by Mike Artell

All rights reserved. If you'd like to use brief quotations or an image from this book for book review purposes, please feel free to do so. For other permissions or usage requests please contact Mike Artell via his website – www.mikeartell.com

Printed in the United States of America

Published by MJA Creative, LLC

Box 3997, Covington, LA  70434

www.mikeartell.com

The information in this book has been fact-checked by an educator with a Master's Degree in Science Education. If you have questions about the accuracy of any information herein, please write the publisher at the address above with your comments and you will receive a prompt reply.

# INTRODUCTION

Skulls are the "containers" that cover and protect the brains of people and animals and help give shape to their faces. Humans have 8 large bones that make up the **cranium**. The brain is located inside the cranium. There are also 14 other bones that give shape to the face. In small children, the bones of the cranium are not yet joined together tightly. It takes about 2 years for those bones to fuse together.

Try this: Press your fingers to your skull. Feel around for the bumps. Many years ago, there were people who claimed they could tell what kind of personality someone had by the bumps on that person's skull. We now know that's silly but today scientists can often determine how someone's face looked by studying the front of their skeletal skull.

In this book, you'll discover that some of the cutest, friendliest animals have skulls that are strange and unlike what you'd expect. Take a close look at the pictures. You'll see "tunnels" within each of the skulls that are passageways for blood vessels and nerves. Pay attention to the size of the spaces for the eyes and the nose. Those spaces can often be clues to the importance of the animal's sense of vision or smell to finding food or to deciding if it is in danger.

One last note – some of the words in this book are underlined in bold type – like the word, "cranium" above in the first paragraph. The glossary in the back of the book has an explanation of each of those words.

Ready to be surprised and amazed? Great! Let's look at some skulls.

# ABOUT THE AUTHOR

Mike Artell is the author of more than 35 children's books – most of which he also illustrated. Mike has written/illustrated books on a wide variety of topics including...

> Outer space
> Weather
> Smelly bugs
> The Paralympic games
> How to draw cartoons
> How kids can create their own books
> Biographies of professional athletes
> Jokes, riddles and tongue twisters
> Picture books
> Lift-the-flap books

Many of Mike's books have won awards including, "Read Aloud Book of the Year."

Each year, Mike visits more than 50 schools across the United States, Europe and Asia and speaks to more than 14,000 students and teachers about how to think, write and draw more creatively. You can see many of Mike's cartooning videos by doing a YouTube search on, "Mike Artell."

Mike was born and raised in New Orleans, Louisiana and has spent most of his life in the area. He's married to Suzie, a former high school teacher and middle school media specialist.

For more information about Mike Artell's school visits, conference presentations, books and videos, visit www.mikeartell.com.

# Skulls Unlimited

Skulls Unlimited cleans, preserves, and articulates (puts together) skulls and skeletons for museums, schools, and collectors around the world ... and they are one of the best in the world at what they do! Skulls Unlimited receives thousands of animals every year. Each animal has to be stripped of meat (by their dermestid beetles), and cleaned and whitened with chemicals. Then each skeleton is slowly put back together bone by bone. Skulls Unlimited never poaches animals or destroys animals just for their bones (they don't support that behavior either). All of their animals come from natural and predator deaths, road kills, food source by-products, and legal hunting and trapping.

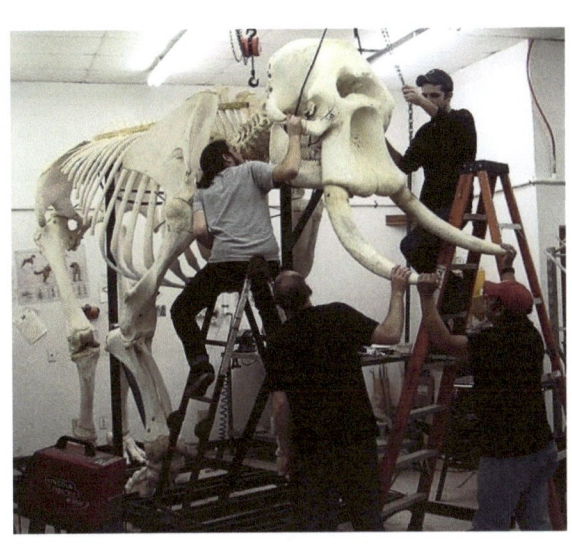

Skulls Unlimited began in 1972 when, at age seven, owner Jay Villemarette found a dog skull. When Jay's father saw his interest, he encouraged Jay to find and collect other skulls. After graduating high school, Jay began selling skulls in his spare time. As sales grew, Jay and his wife Kim began to clean skulls in their kitchen. Starting with only one-page of products in 1986, they turned this unusual hobby into a business. Today, Skulls Unlimited is known worldwide for having the largest variety of skulls and skeletons anywhere!

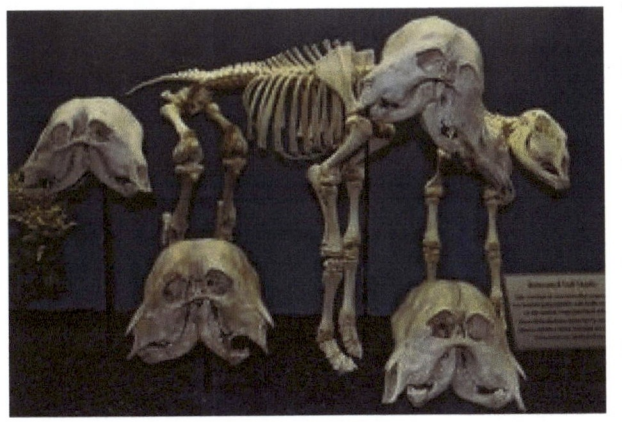

In 2010, Jay's dream of opening a skeleton museum became a reality. The Museum of Osteology in Oklahoma City currently has hundreds of skulls and skeletons on display and is one of the largest private collections of skulls and skeletons in the United States. And in 2015, Skulls Unlimited opened its second museum, Skeletons, in Orlando, Florida.

Skulls Unlimited provides educational classes and outreach programs for schools and the community. For more information, contact:

SKULLS UNLIMITED INTERNATIONAL, INC.
10313 South Sunnylane   Oklahoma City, OK 73160
www.skullsunlimited.com  1-800-659-SKULL (7585)

# Table of contents

Alligator ............................................. 8

Armadillo ........................................ 10

Aye-Aye............................................ 12

Babirusa ......................................... 14

Bat..................................................... 16

Beaver.............................................. 18

Boxer................................................ 20

Eagle ................................................ 22

Elephant.......................................... 24

Fox .................................................... 26

Gorilla .............................................. 28

Hippopotamus .............................. 30

Hyena............................................... 32

Kangaroo .................................................. 34

King Mackerel ........................................ 36

Llama ...................................................... 38

Piranha ................................................... 40

Rabbit ..................................................... 42

Raccoon ................................................. 44

Rattlesnake ............................................ 46

Shoebill .................................................. 48

Tiger ....................................................... 50

Water monitor ....................................... 52

Zebra ...................................................... 54

Skull match ............................................ 56

Glossary ................................................. 57

Want more information? ................... 58

# ALLIGATOR

Scientific name: *Alligator mississippiensis*

The American Alligator is the largest reptile in North America. The average male alligator grows to about 15 feet (4.6 meters) and the average female grows to about 9.8 feet (3 meters) in length. Although these reptiles are not as aggressive as crocodiles, they will attack if they feel threatened.

In 1956, the song, "SEE YOU LATER, ALLIGATOR" was a big hit for the band, "Bill Haley and the Comets."

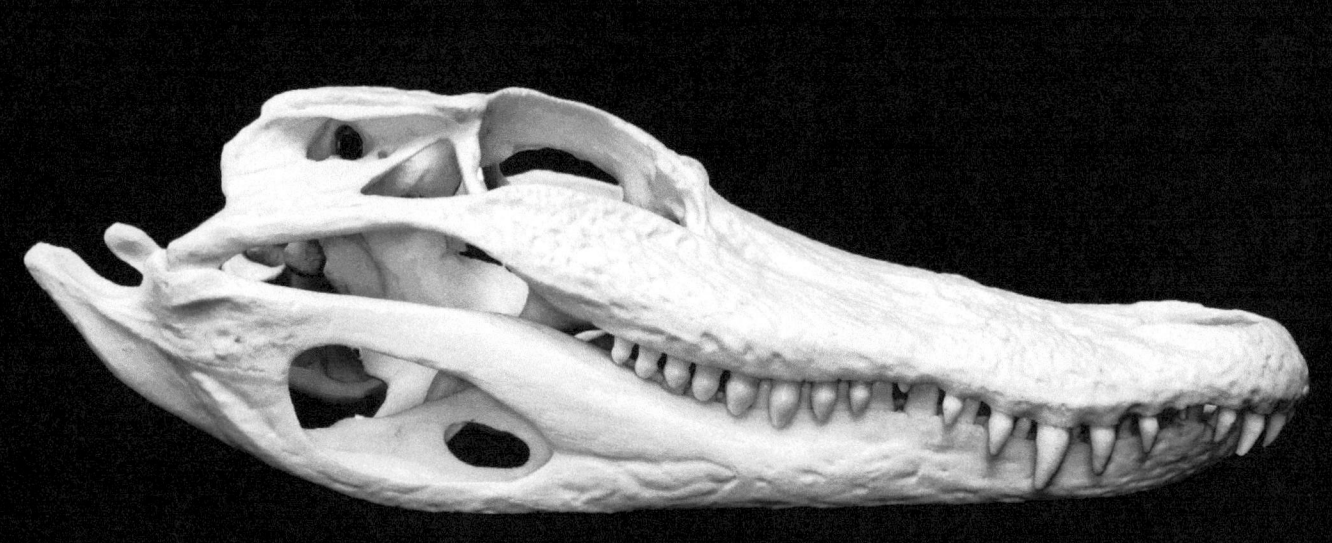

# ARMADILLO

(Nine-banded armadillo)
Scientific name: *Dasypus novemcinctus*

The nine-banded armadillo is the only armadillo found in the United States. It has too many armored plates to be able to roll up into a ball. Only the three-banded armadillo can do that.

Female armadillos always give birth to four identical babies —either four females or four males.

The nine-banded armadillo can hold its breath for almost 6 minutes.

**How high can *you* jump?**
A nine-banded armadillo can jump about three to four feet straight up in the air.

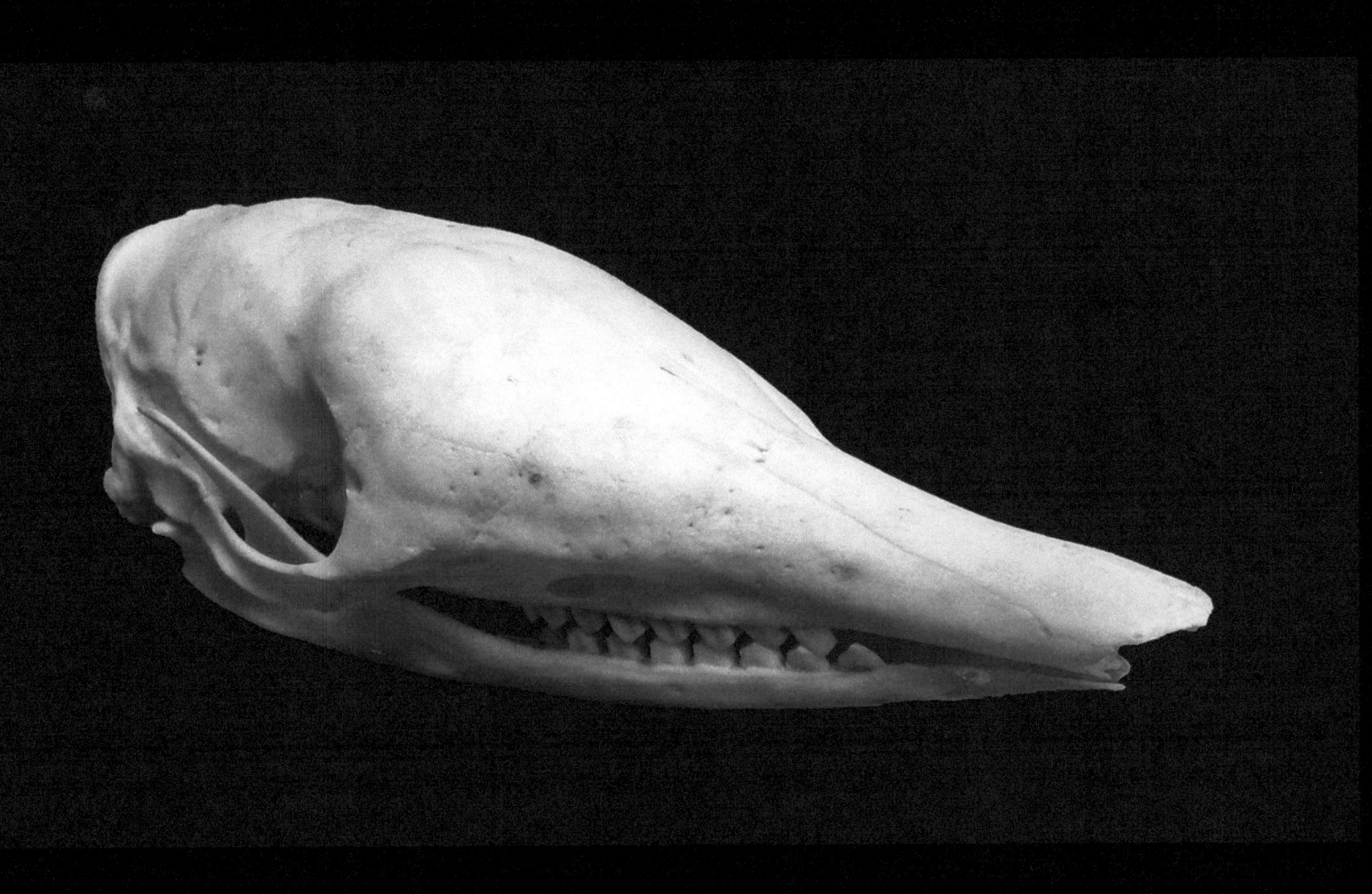

# AYE-AYE

Scientific name: *Daubentonia madagascariensis*

When scientists first saw the Aye-Aye they thought it was a type of squirrel. But it's really a type of lemur. The Aye-Aye is the largest **nocturnal** primate in the world. The average male weighs about 6 pounds (2.7 kilograms). Females weigh about 5 ½ pounds (2.5 kilograms).

Aye-Aye uses its weird, skinny middle finger to tap quickly on a branch or log. The Aye-Aye can tell by the sound if there are fat, juicy bugs inside. If the sound is right, the Aye-Aye uses its sharp front teeth to chew into the branch or log. Then (and this is the creepy part), the Aye-Aye puts its long, weird finger into the opening, digs out the bugs and pops them into its mouth. Yum!

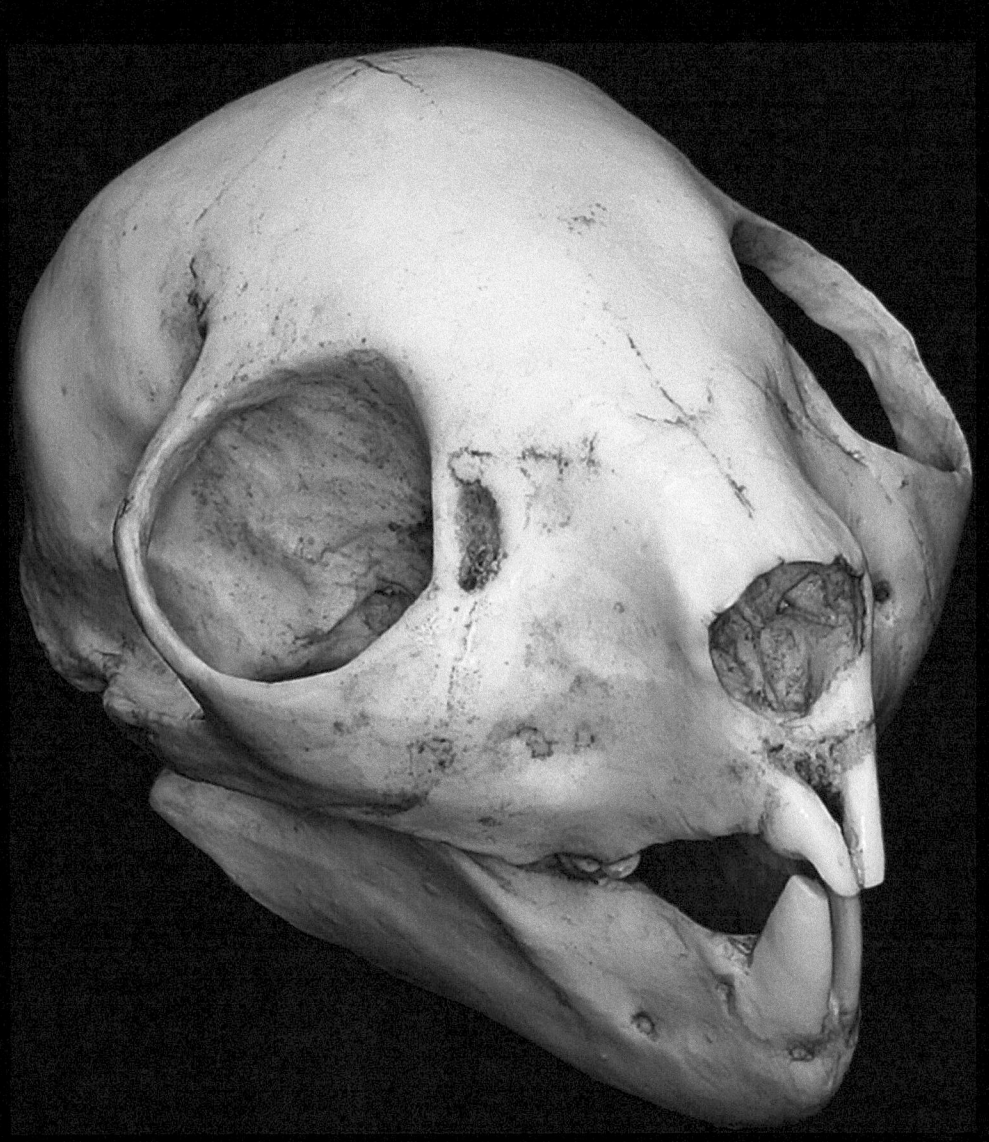

# BABIRUSA

Scientific name: *Babyrousa celebensis*

Babirusas are **omnivorous** and will eat just about anything. The oddest thing about male babirusas is their upper canine teeth. They curl up out of the babirusa's mouth, over Its forehead and down toward its skull.

At first, you might think that the babirusa uses those teeth for fighting but that's not the case. The teeth are brittle and would break quickly in a fight. That's not the way babirusas fight anyway. When babirusas fight, they stand up on their back legs and punch like two really chubby boxers. The fact is, scientists aren't quite sure what the purpose of the amazing upper teeth are. They might be there just to impress female babirusas.

Babirusas are also known as, "pig deer."

How insulting!!

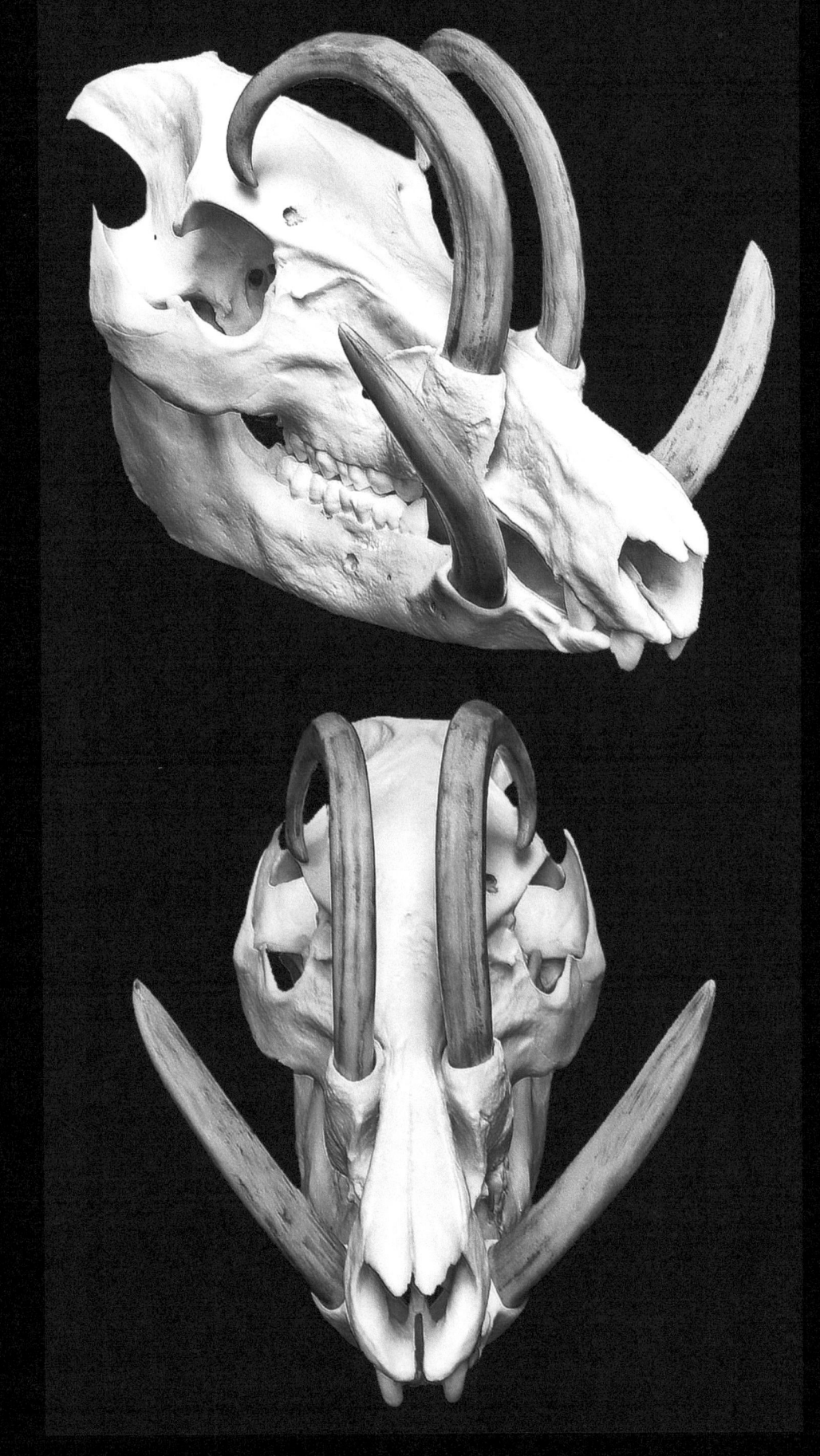

# BAT

(Egyptian Fruit Bat)
Scientific name: *Rousettus aegyptiacus*

Egyptian fruit bats are about 6 inches (15.2 centimeters) long and have a wing span of about 2 feet (61 centimeters). Their faces look similar to the face of a dog or a fox. That's how they got the nickname, "flying fox." And don't worry...these bats won't suck your blood. They're **frugivorous**. That means they only eat fruit.

The first **Batman** comic was published in 1940.

**It's true!** Bats are the only mammals that can fly.

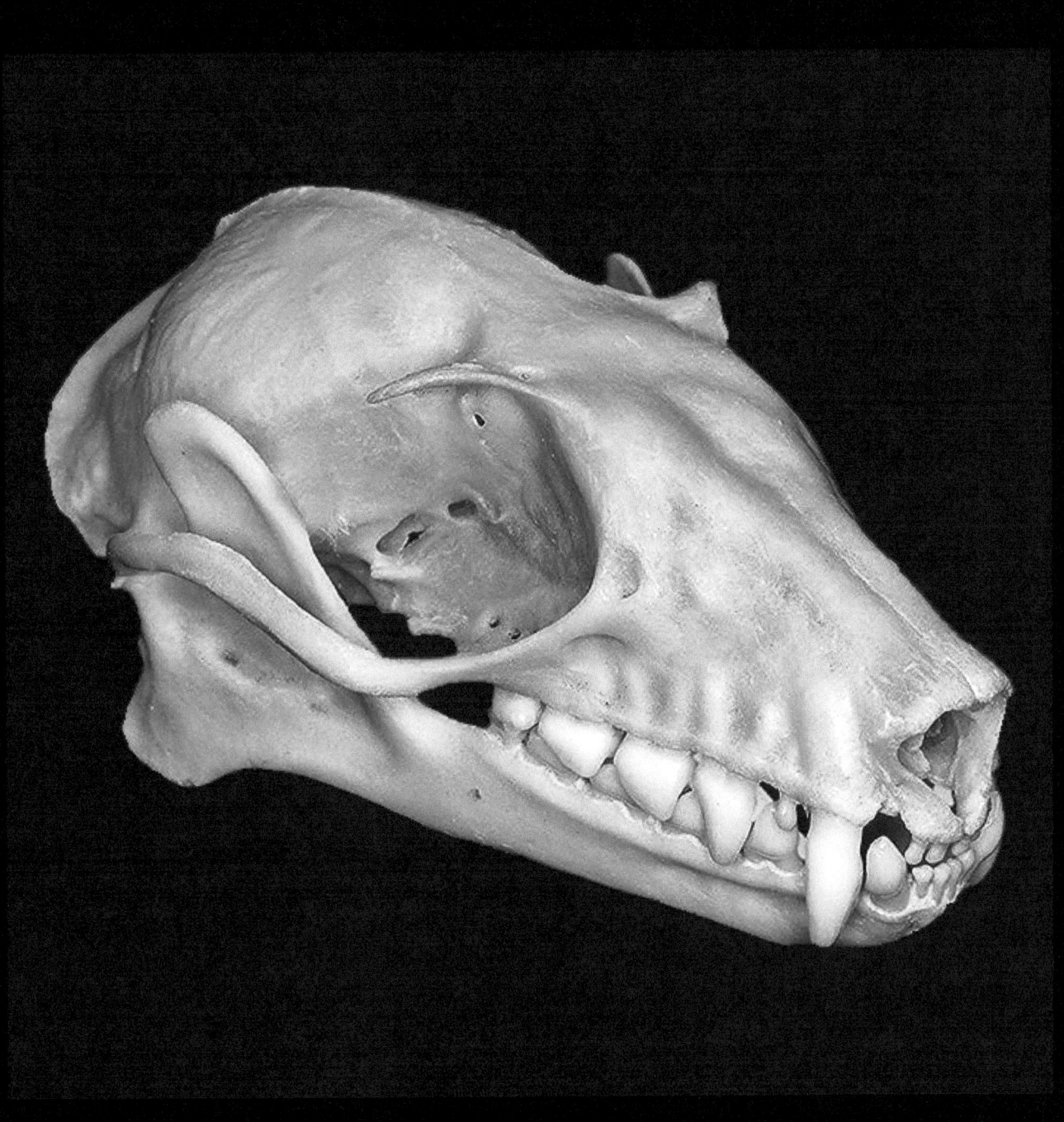

# BEAVER

(North American Beaver)
Scientific name: *Castor canadensis*

When beavers sense danger they slap their tails on the water as a warning to other beavers in the colony. Beavers' front teeth never stop growing so they constantly chew on things to keep their teeth from getting too long.

Beavers are nocturnal animals.

### Beaver **idiom**
A person who is an, "eager beaver" is someone who is full of energy and works hard.

The states of Alaska, Ohio, Oregon, Pennsylvania, Utah, Washington, West Virginia and Wisconsin all have cities named Beaver.

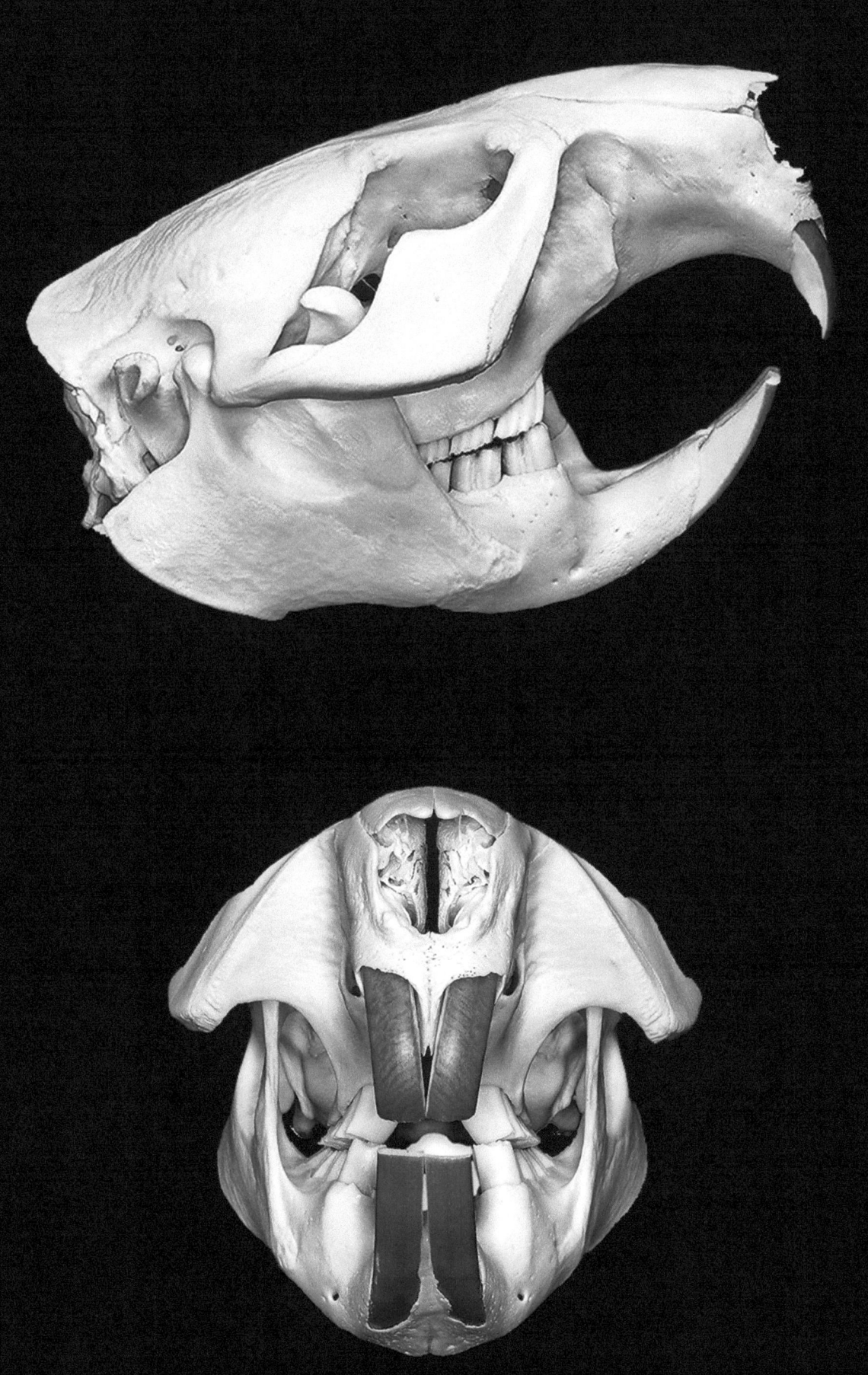

# BOXER

Scientific name: *Canis lupus familiaris*

Boxers are strong, energetic, intelligent dogs. Because of this, the U. S. military has used them as guard dogs and messenger dogs. They also make great pets and are very loyal to their owners. At dog shows, boxers are part of the group of dogs known as the "Working Group."

Boxers are usually brownish with white markings. The white markings are called "flash."

Boxers are wonderful dogs but they do have a few unpleasant habits. They tend to snore, they drool a lot and they're famous for…um…passing gas.

# EAGLE

(Bald eagle)
Scientific name: *Haliaeetus leucocephalus*

Bald eagles aren't really bald. The word, "bald" once meant "white-headed." The bald eagle was officially adopted as the emblem of the United States in 1787. It can be seen on the Great Seal which is added to official documents, such as passports.

After the condor, the bald eagle is the largest bird of prey in North America.

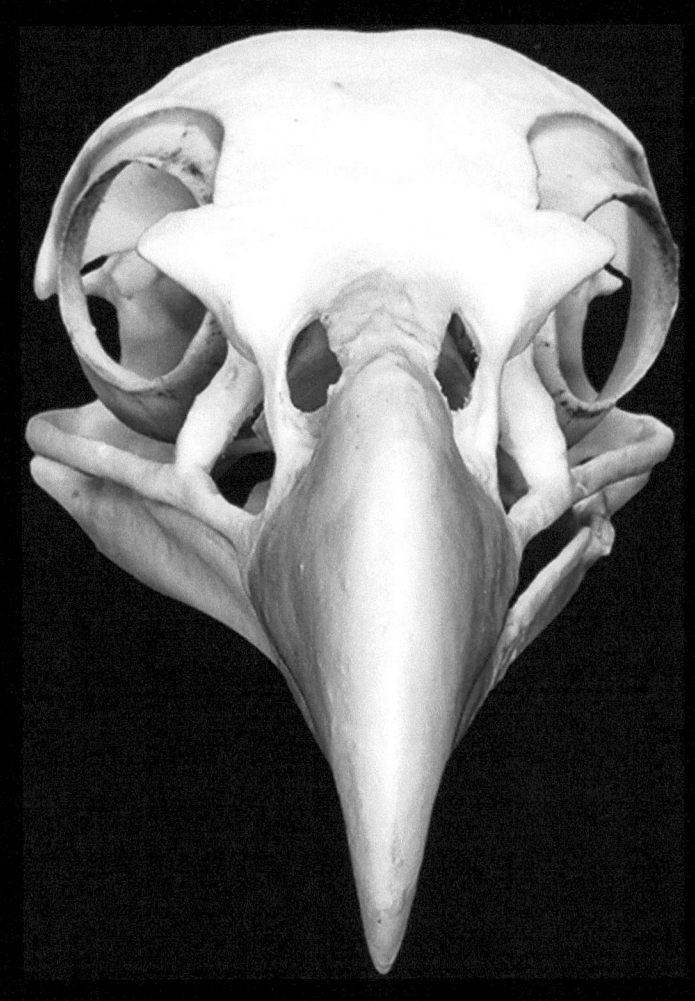
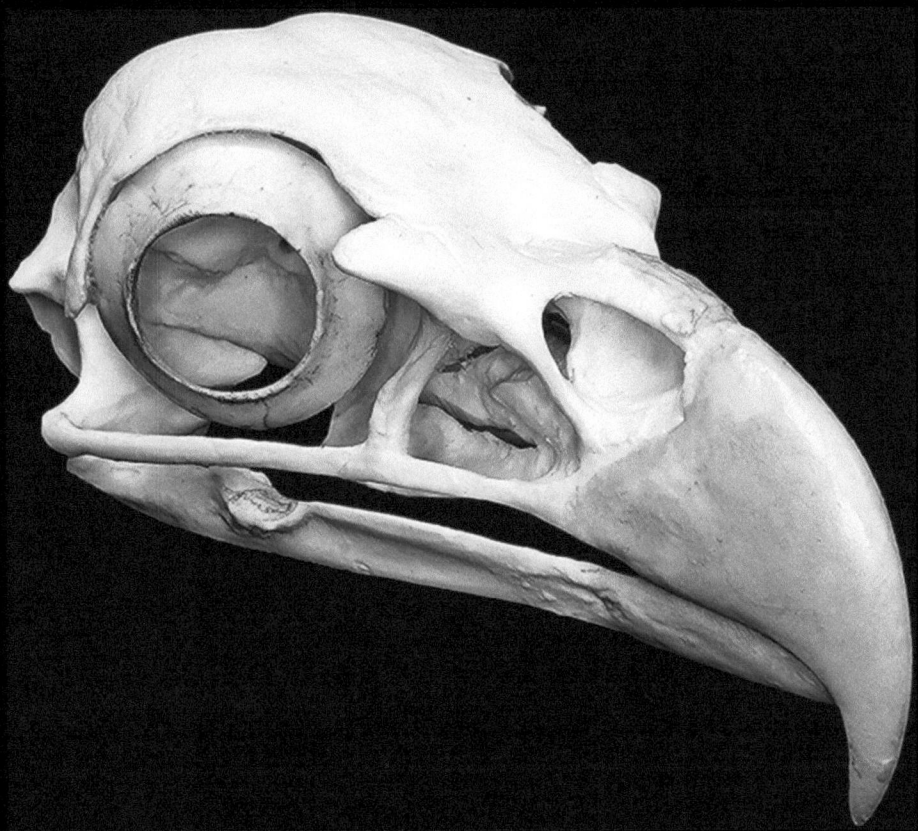

# ELEPHANT

(African Elephant)
Scientific name: *Loxodonta africana*

Elephants can pick up small objects with their noses, which is a pretty cool trick. But do you know something elephants CAN'T do? They can't JUMP! They're just too big and heavy.

Elephants are good swimmers and they can run fast - about 25 miles per hour (40 kilometers per hour) but they usually don't have to. Adult elephants don't have any natural enemies in the wild so they can take their time (about 16 hours every day) eating grasses, leaves and roots.

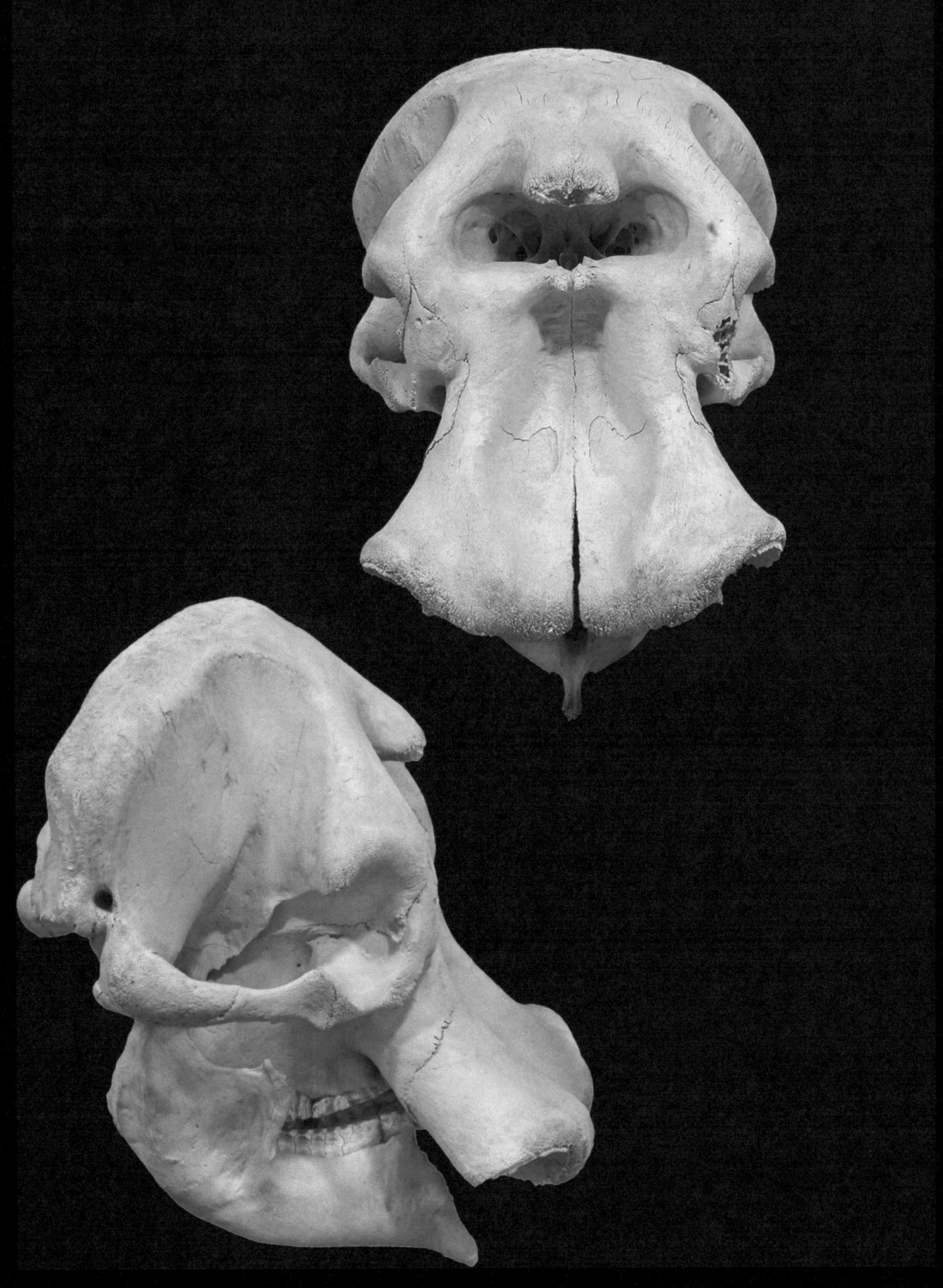

# FOX

(Bat-eared fox)
Scientific name: *Otocyon megalotis*

Imagine you were an animal that ate mostly termites. Now imagine that the best way to find those termites was to listen for the sounds they made when they are eating. Would it be helpful to have REALLY big ears and great hearing? You bet it would! That's why the bat-eared fox is so good at finding food.

The scientific name for the bat-eared fox is *Otocyon megalotis*. The word, "otocyon" comes from the Greek words for ear (otus) and dog (cyon). The word, "megalotis" comes from the Greek words for large (mega) and ear (otus). "Dog with big ears." Get it?

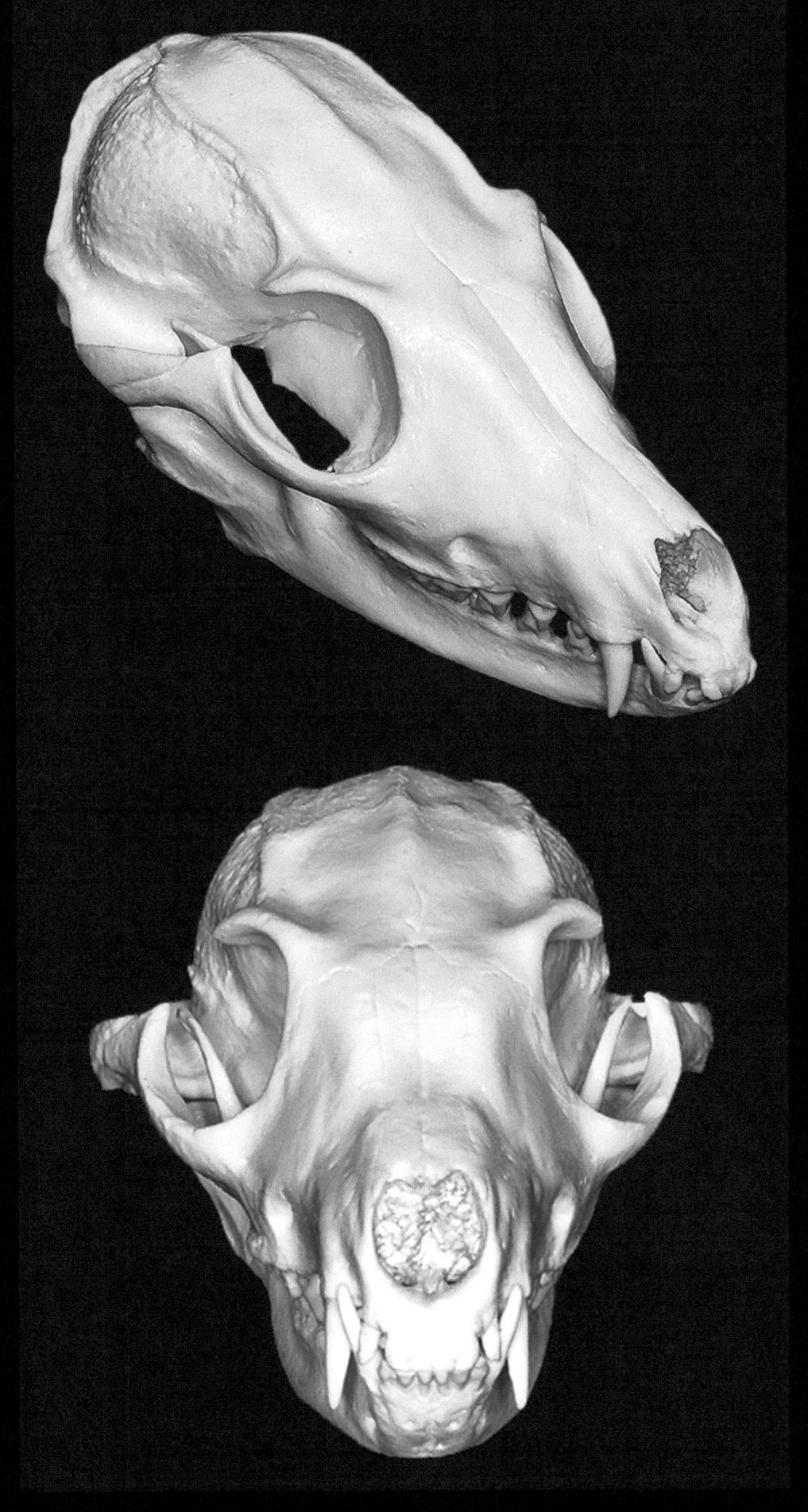

# GORILLA

(Lowland Gorilla)
Scientific name: *Gorilla gorilla gorilla*

Gorillas are highly intelligent **primates**. The males can grow as tall as 6 feet (1.8 meters) and although they can walk upright on two legs, they prefer to walk bent over using all four limbs. Gorillas have very large stomachs. Their **intestines** need to be large to digest all the leaves and plants they eat every day. Gorillas spend most of their lives on the ground and make a new nest to sleep in every night.

"King Kong" was a movie about a fictional gorilla. The first King Kong movie appeared in theaters in 1933. Several other versions of the movie have been made since then.

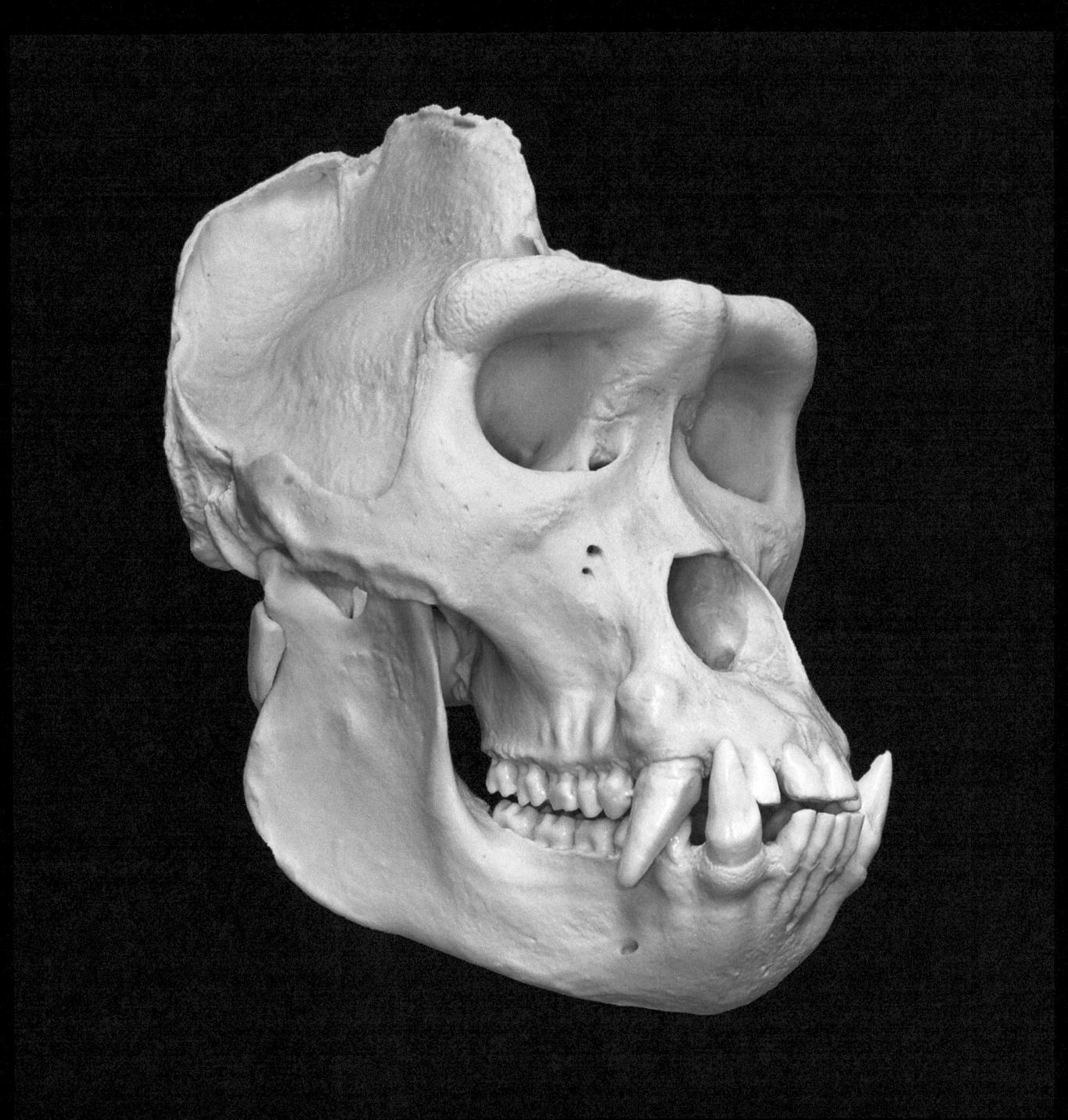

# HIPPOPOTAMUS

Scientific name: *Hippopotamus amphibius*

The word, "hippopotamus" comes from two Greek words meaning, "river horse." But what the ancient Greeks did not know was that the hippo's closest relatives are not horses but <u>cetaceans</u> – such as whales and porpoises. Hippos are one of the most dangerous animals in the world because they are so aggressive.

Hippos spend most of their time relaxing in the water or near river banks. To keep from getting sunburned, their skin produces a red liquid sometimes called, "blood sweat." It's not blood or sweat. It's just the hippo's version of sunscreen. When hippos feel threatened, they will open their huge mouths and display their gigantic teeth.

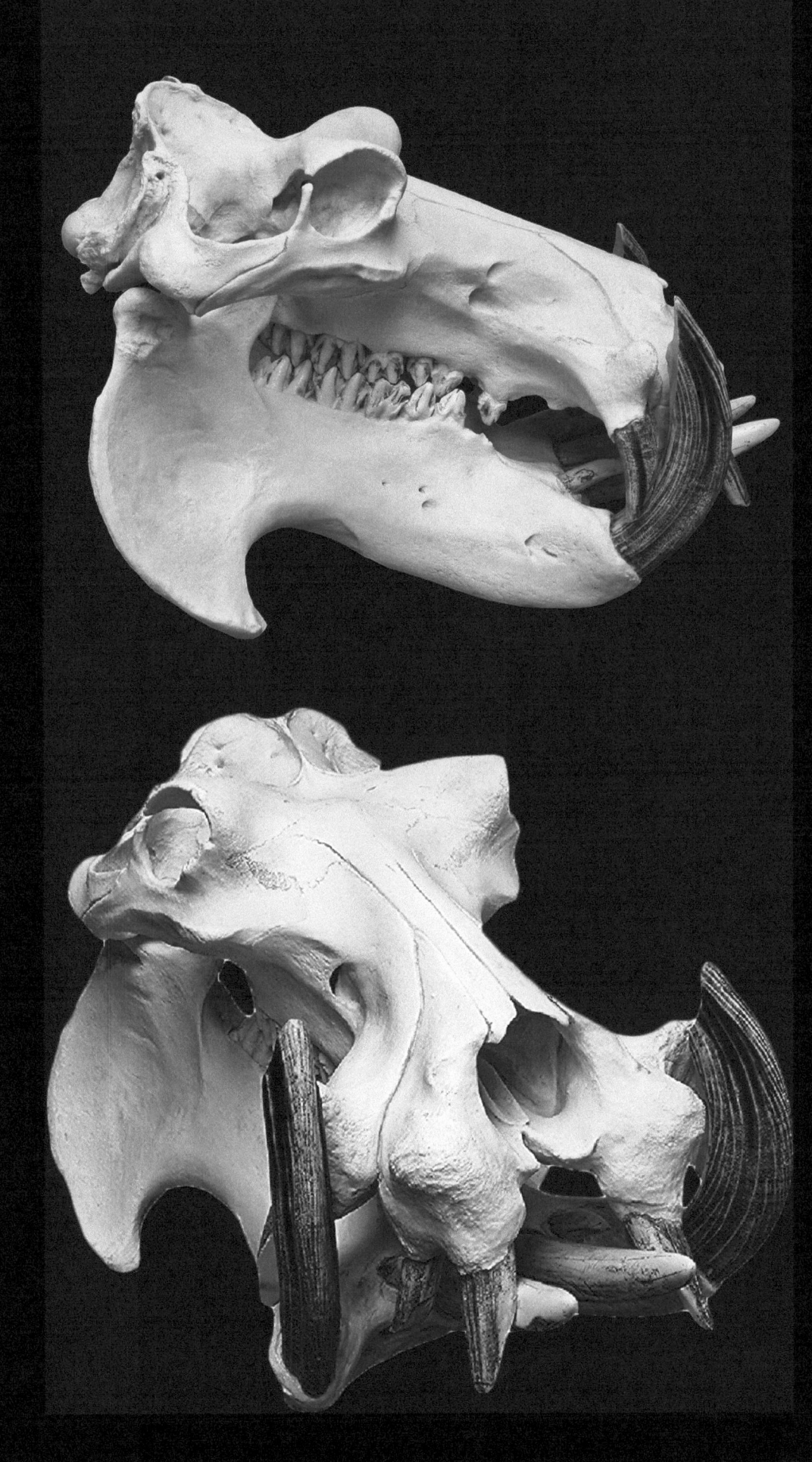

# HYENA

(Striped hyena)
Scientific name: *Hyaena hyaena*

Striped hyenas are active at night. They are omnivores and will eat plants, fruit and other animals. They are also happy to eat the remains of animals that have been the victims of other predators. In populated areas, they will often feed on the scraps in garbage dumps. When they feel threatened, hyenas will raise the hair on their necks and backs. This makes them look much larger and more dangerous.

The striped hyena is closely related to the spotted hyena which is sometimes called the, "laughing hyena." It's called that because of the strange calls it makes when it communicates with other spotted hyenas.

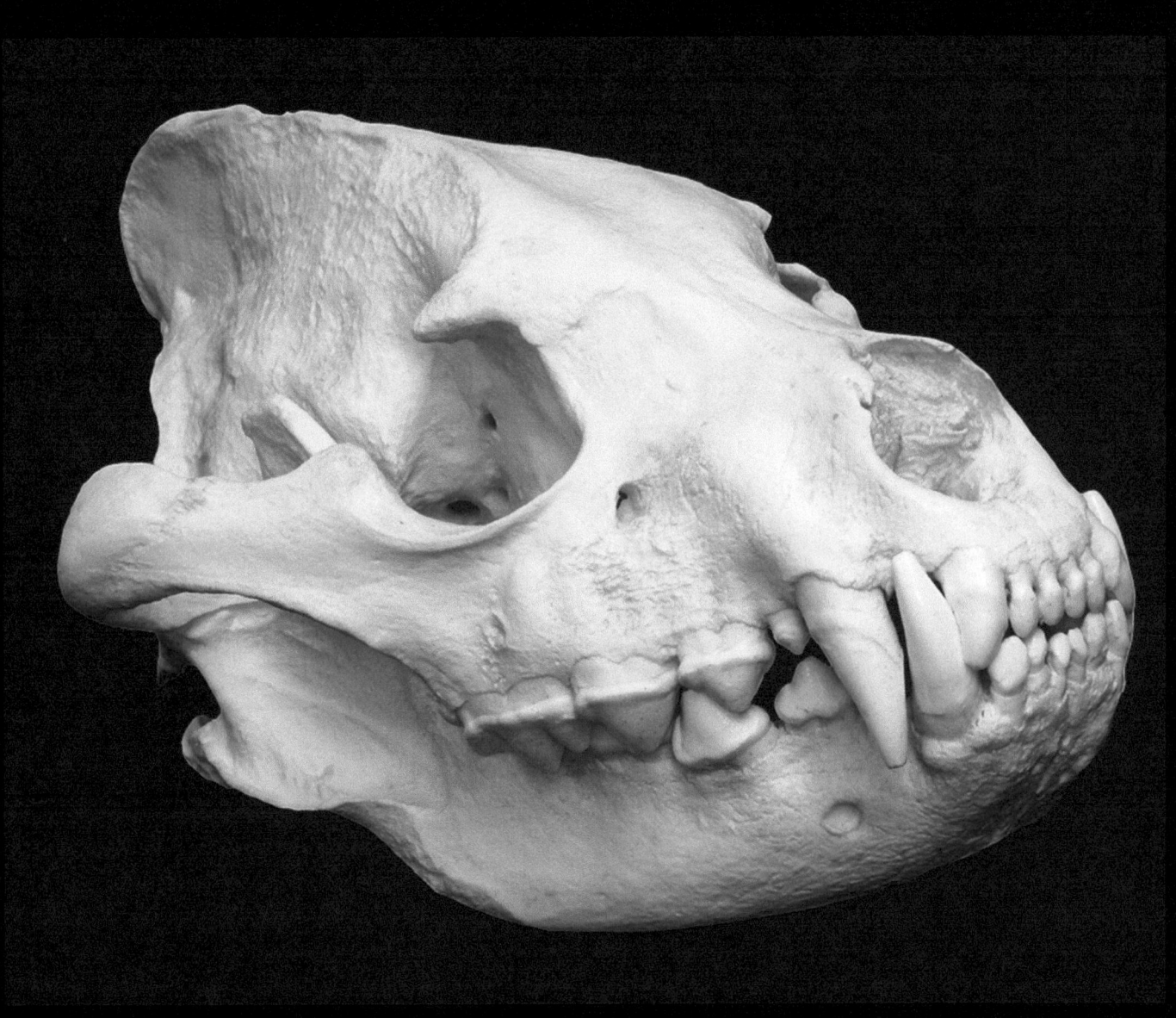

# Kangaroo

(Red Kangaroo)
Scientific name: *Macropus rufus*

The red kangaroo is the largest **marsupial** in the world. It can jump nearly 10 feet (3 meters) in the air and about 25 feet (7.6 meters) forward. But don't ask a red kangaroo to walk backwards – it can't because of its long tail and large back legs. A group of kangaroos is called a "mob" and baby kangaroos are called "joeys."

Sometimes, kangaroos will "box" each other by sitting back on their tails, kicking with their feet and "punching" with their front paws.

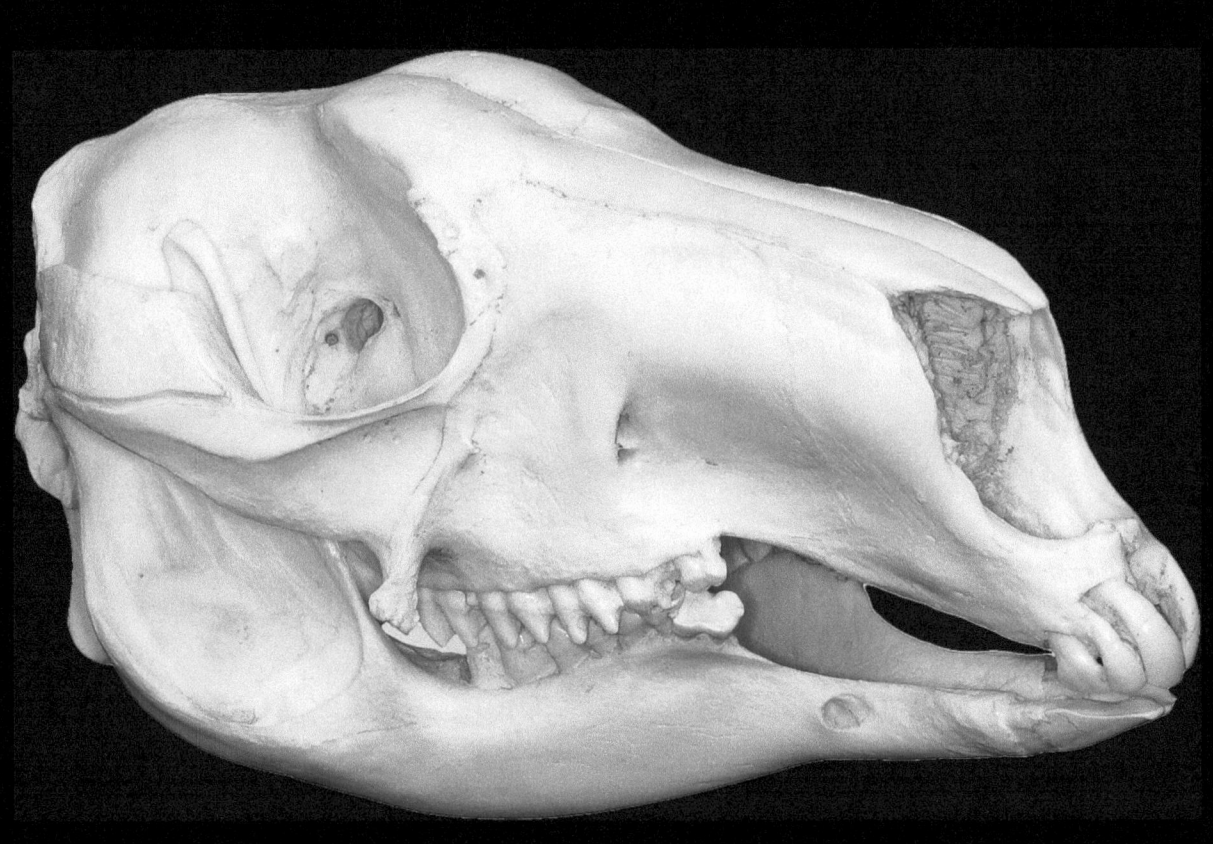

# LLAMA

Scientific name: *Lama glama*

Llamas are members of the camel family. In the country of Peru, llamas are used as pack animals because they are strong and sure-footed. Llamas are very smart - when a llama thinks that the weight on its back is too heavy, it simply lies down and refuses to move. Llama wool is used to make clothes, blankets, rugs and ropes.

Llama body parts: 1 ears – 2 poll – 3 withers – 4 back – 5 hip – 6 croup – 7 base of tail – 8 tail – 9 buttock – 10 hock – 11 metatarsal gland – 12 heel – 13 cannon bone – 14 gaskin – 15 stifle joint – 16 flank – 17 barrel – 18 elbow – 19 pastern – 20 fetlock – 21 Knee – 22 Chest – 23 point of shoulder – 24 shoulder – 25 throat – 26 cheek or jowl – 27 muzzle

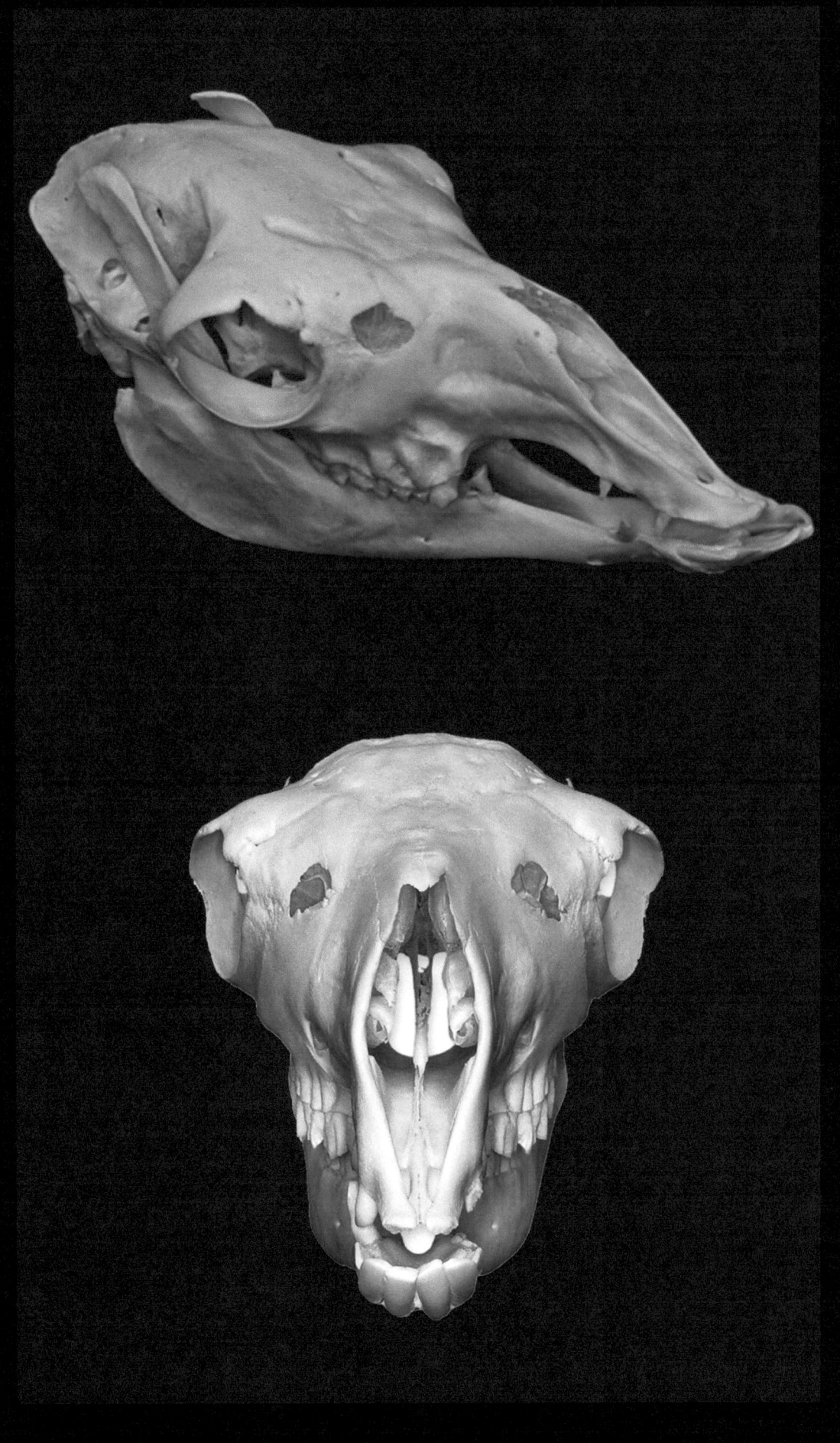

# MACKEREL

(King mackerel)

Scientific name: *Scomberomorus cavalla*

King mackerel are members of the tuna family. They prefer warm water and travel in schools. The average adult king mackerel weighs about 30 pounds (14 kilograms), but they can grow almost three times that size. They are a popular food fish and are very high in protein.

King mackerel are also known as, "kingfish." Huey Long's nickname was, "The Kingfish." Huey Long was governor of the state of Louisiana from 1928 to 1932. He was also a United States Senator from Louisiana from 1932 to 1935.

You might hear someone say, "Holy Mackerel!" when they are surprised. That's an old expression which means the same thing as, "Oh, my gosh!"

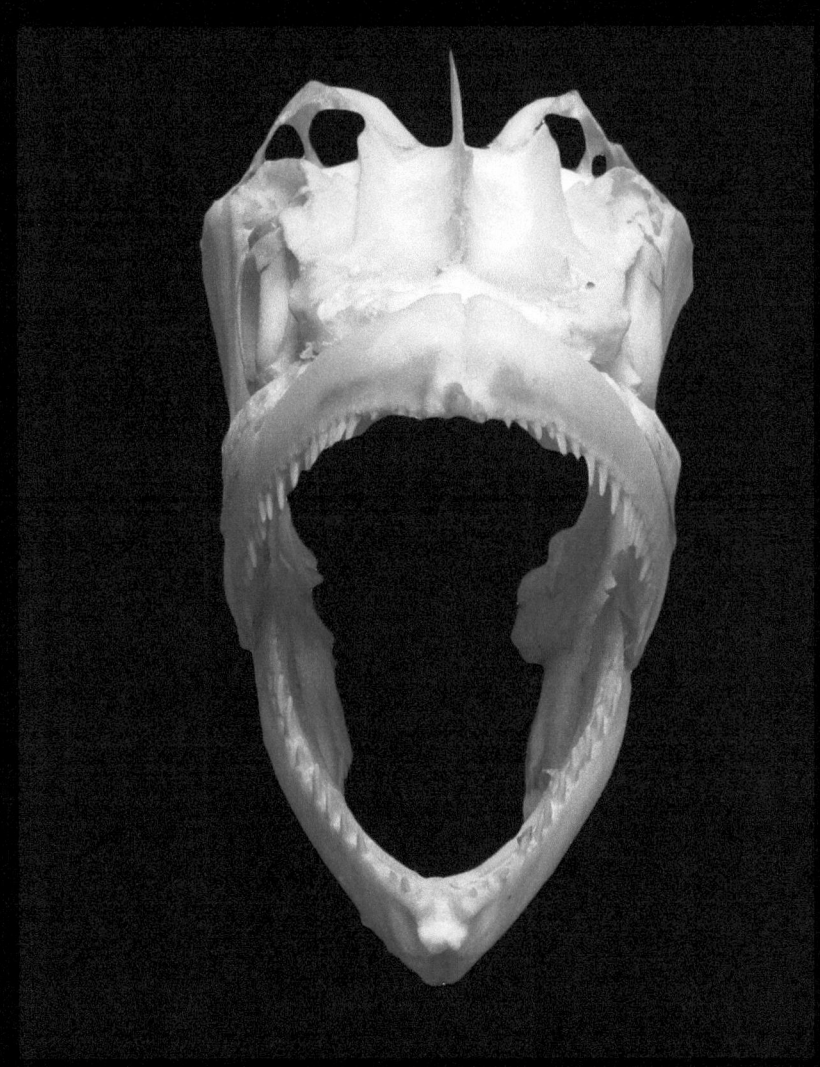

# PIRANHA

Scientific name: *Pygocentrus nattereri*

The word, "piranha" comes from two Brazilian Tupi Indian words. The first is, "pira" which means, "fish." The second is, "ranha" which means, "tooth."

Piranhas have one row of very sharp teeth on each jaw and in the dry season when water levels fall, schools of piranhas can become very aggressive.

"By the way...be careful. My fish bites."

Piranhas vary in size from about 5.5 inches to 10.25 inches (14 centimeters to 26 centimeters) long. Many states do not allow people to keep piranhas as pets.

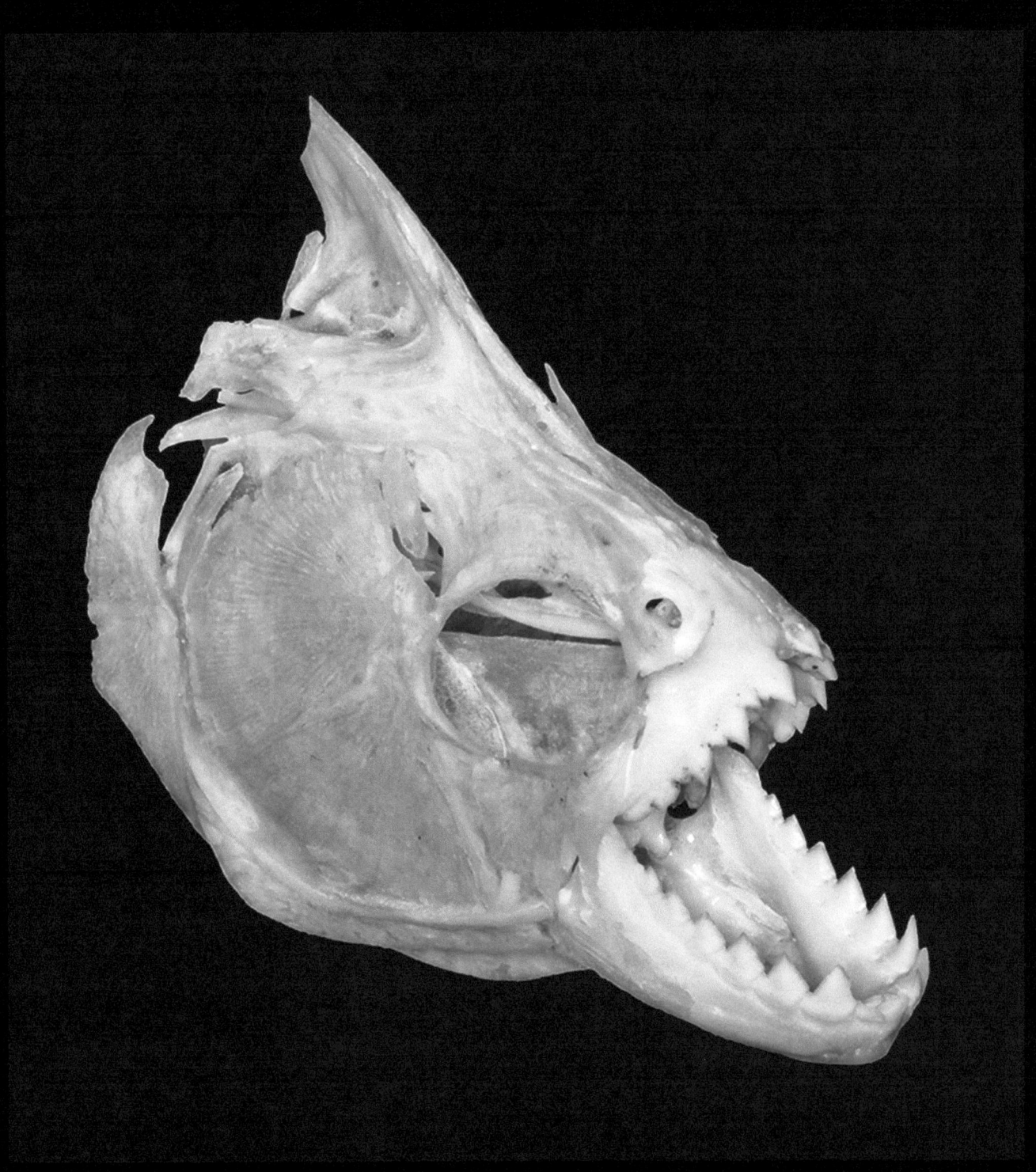

# RABBIT

(Eastern Cottontail)
Scientific name: *Sylvilagus floridanus*

Cottontail rabbits are **crepuscular** animals. On windy days, cottontail rabbits usually stay in their burrows. Why? Because the wind rustles the trees and grass and it makes it harder for them to hear any predators that might be approaching.

Two of the most famous rabbits in children's literature are Peter Rabbit who was the main character in the story, Peter Rabbit by Beatrix Potter and The White Rabbit from Alice in Wonderland, written by Lewis Carroll.

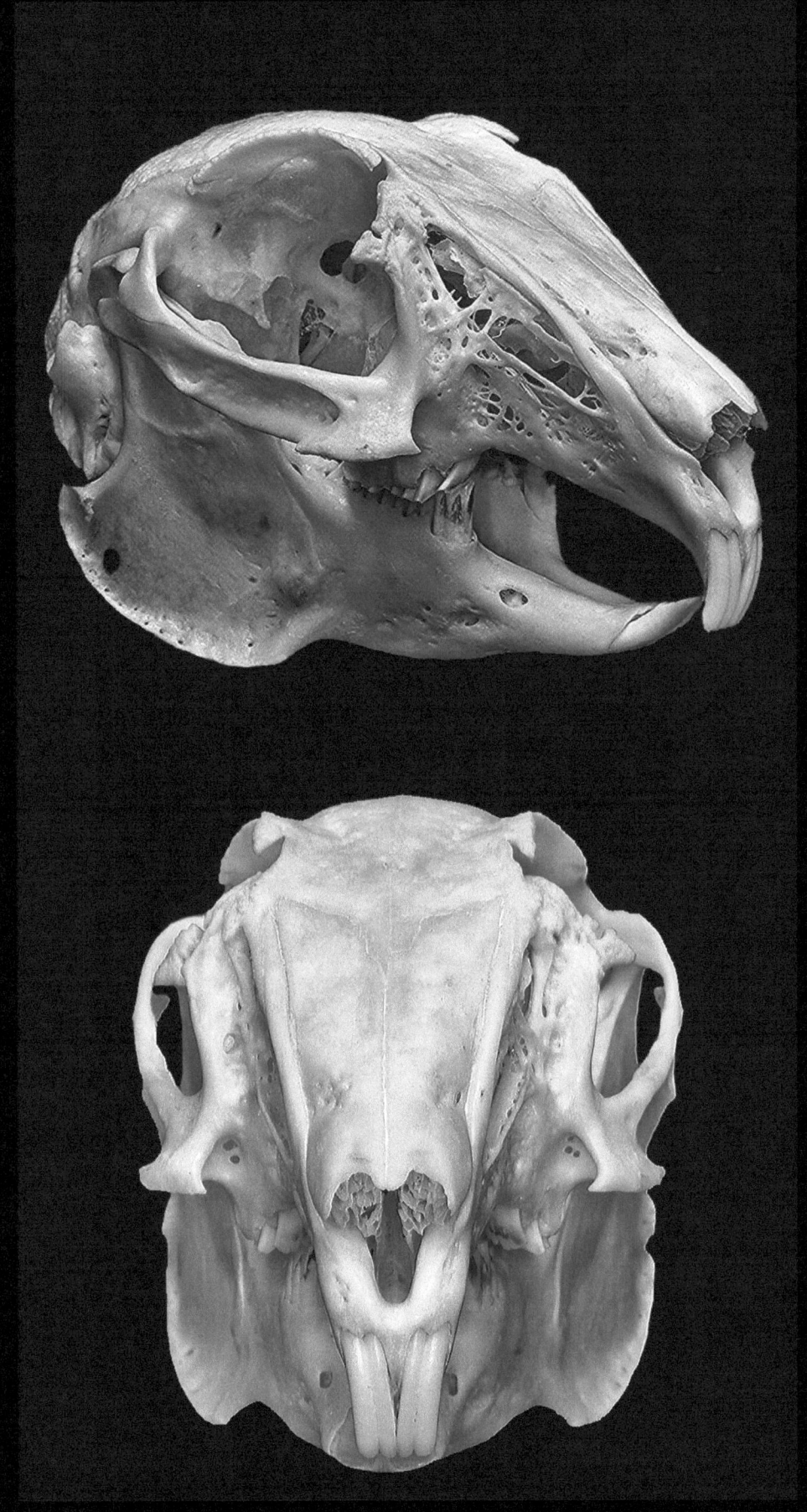

# Raccoon

Scientific name: *Procyon lotor*

Raccoons have an incredible sense of touch. The palms of their front paws are covered with a hard layer of cells which become soft in water. Raccoons are often seen at the edge of rivers or ponds looking for food. They rub the food they find which makes it look as though they're washing it.

Raccoons can also do something very special with their back feet. They can actually rotate them so they're pointing backwards. That way, they can climb down trees face-first.

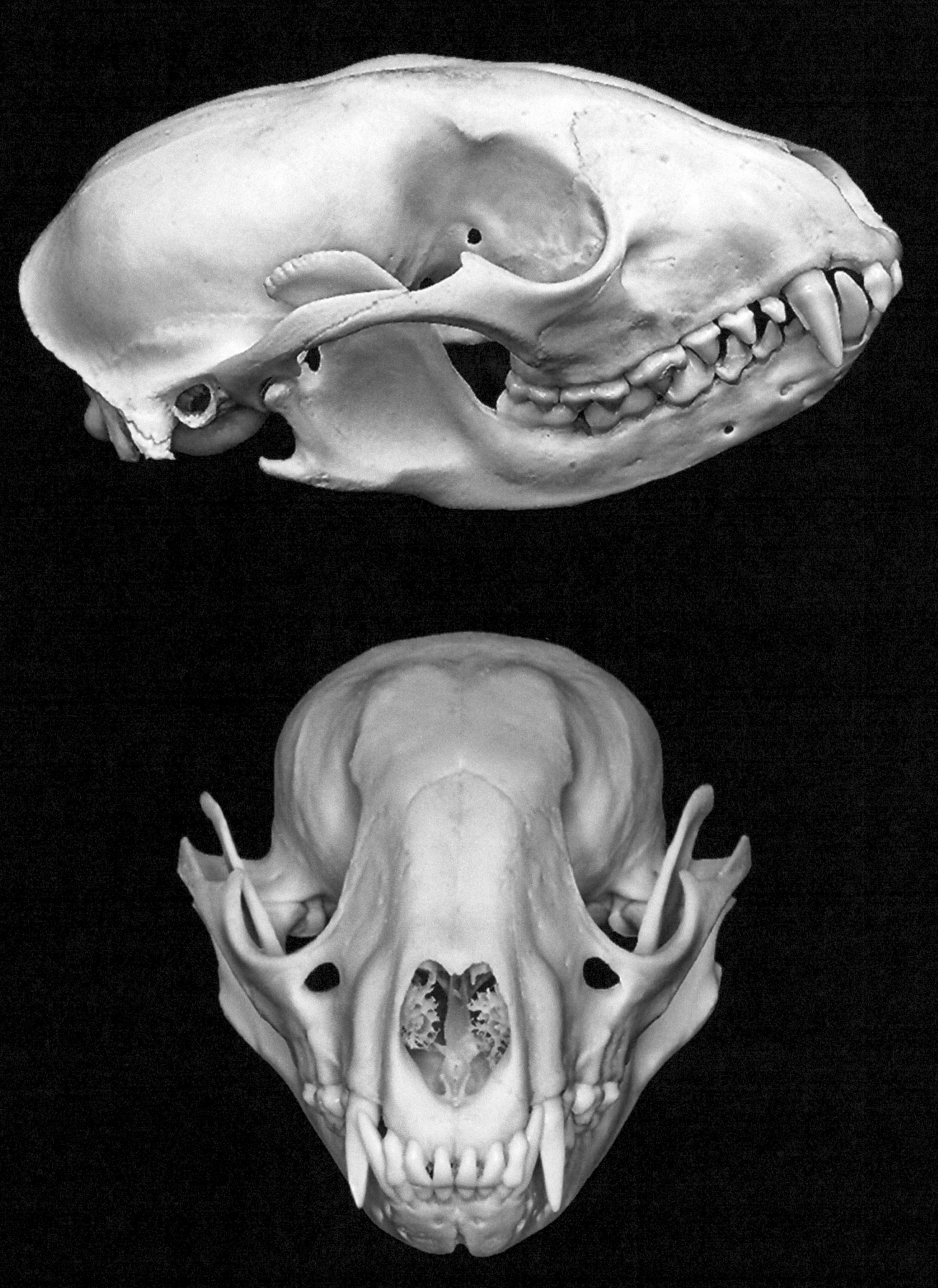

# RATTLESNAKE

(Western Diamondback)
Scientific name: *Crotalus atrox*

A rattlesnake's "rattler" is made of interlocking segments that are loosely connected. Some people used to believe that you could tell how old a rattlesnake was by counting the number of segments. But that's not true. The segments are brittle and sometimes break off so that's not a reliable way of determining a rattlesnake's age.

An average diamondback weighs 4 - 6 pounds (1.8 to 2.7 kg) and grows to a length of about 4 feet (1.2 meters). Adult males are much larger than adult females. Along with their cousin, the Eastern Diamondback Rattlesnake (*Crotalus adamanteus*), they are responsible for most of the fatal snake bites in the United States each year.

There is a professional baseball team called, The Arizona Diamondbacks.

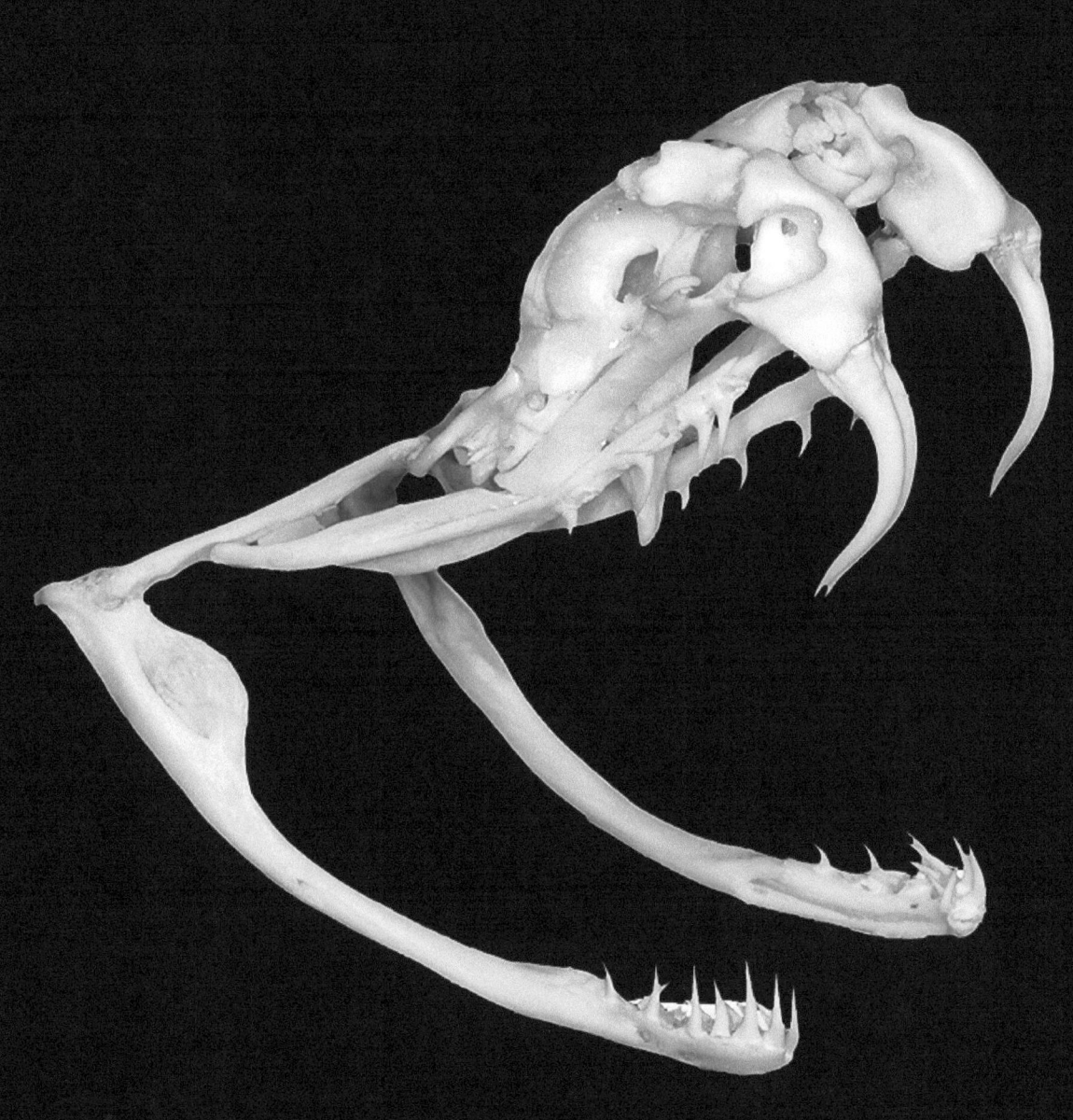

# SHOEBILL

Scientific name: *Balaeniceps rex*

It's not hard to see why this large, African bird is called a, "shoebill." Its beak looks a lot like a wooden clog shoe. The shoebill is known for moving very slowly and also very quickly. When hunting, it will walk very slowly or stand perfectly still in shallow water for long periods of time. Then when it sees something to eat… ZAP! It thrusts its beak lightning fast into the water and (hopefully) comes up with a tasty lungfish – its favorite food. Some people call the shoebill a, "shoebill stork," but the shoebill is actually more closely related to pelicans and herons.

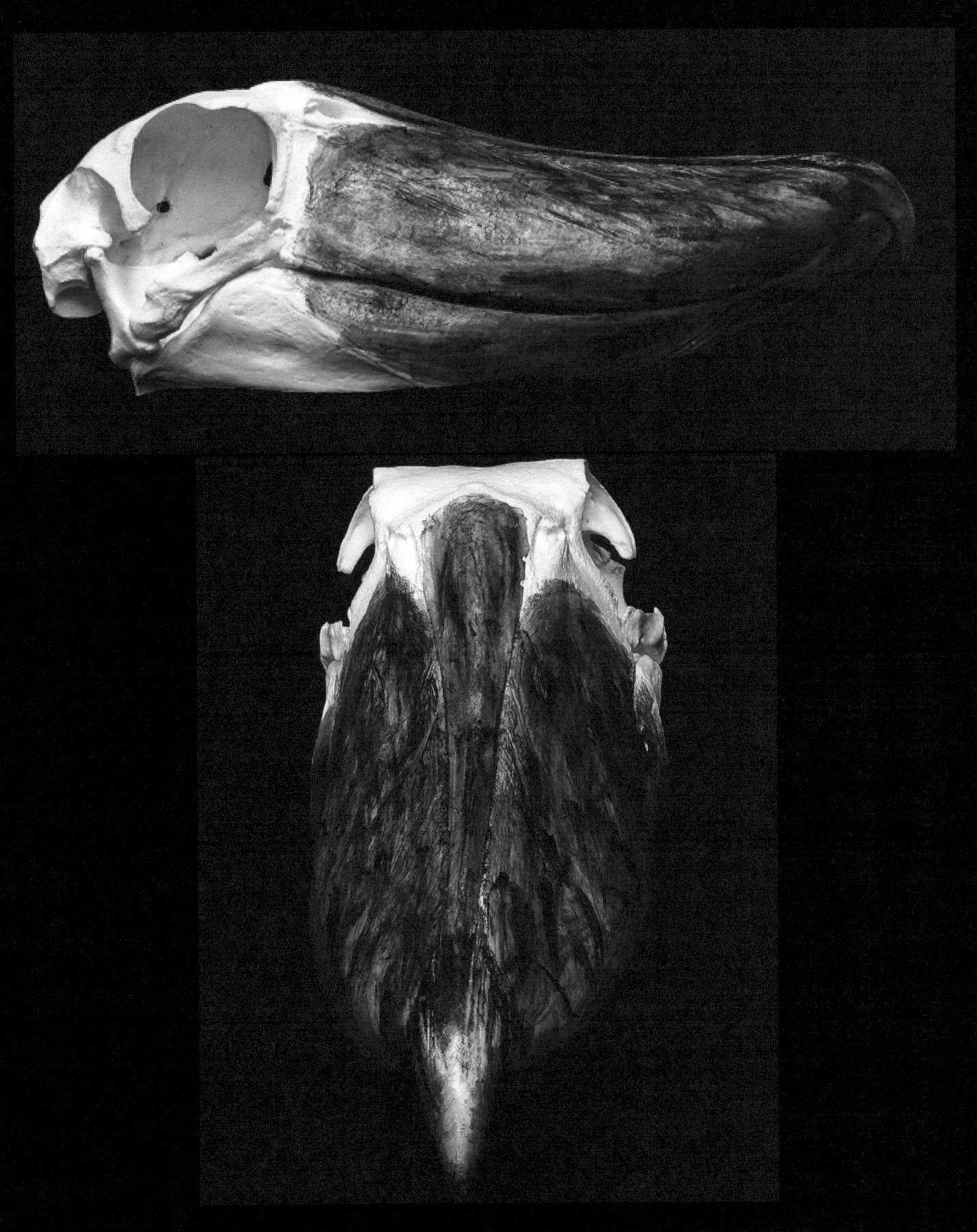

# TIGER

(Bengal tiger)
Scientific name: *Panthera tigris*

Tigers are the biggest cats (Yes, they're bigger than lions). Unlike many cats, tigers like the water and are good swimmers. Tigers often sneak up on their prey and attack them from the rear or side. Unfortunately (for the tiger), this doesn't always work. A tiger has a successful hunt only about once every ten times it tries.

The Spanish word for tiger is, "tigre."

During World War II there was a group of pilots known as, "The Flying Tigers."

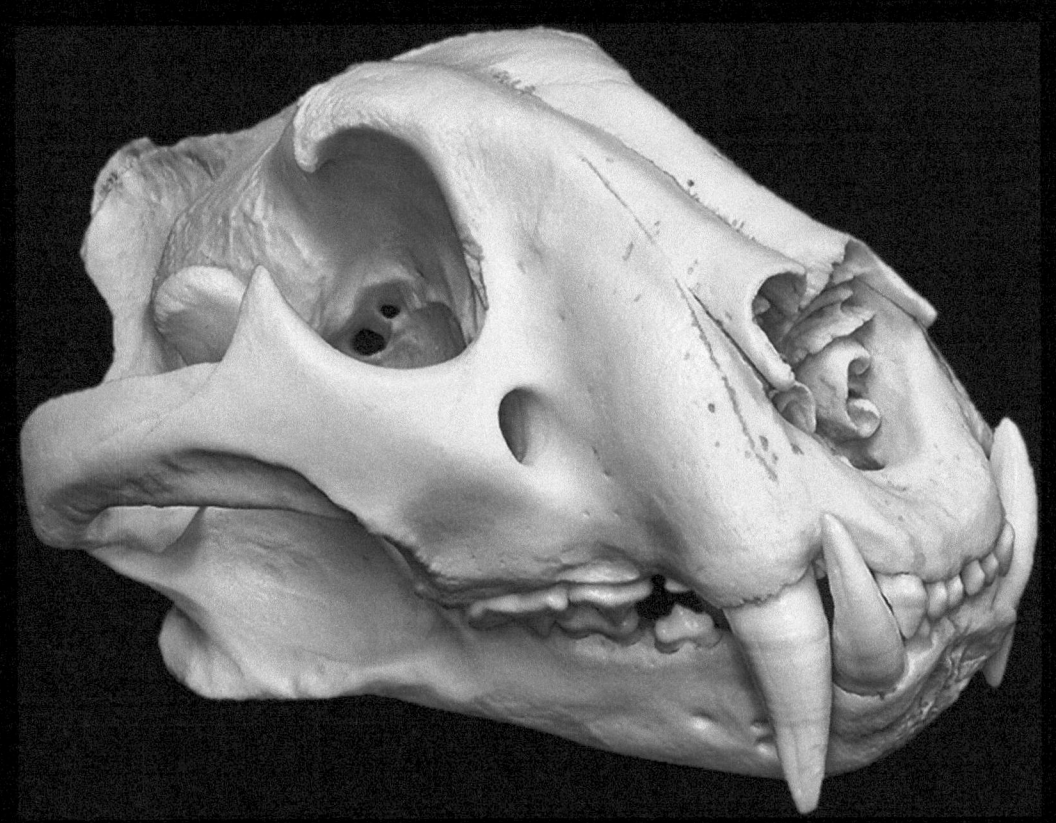
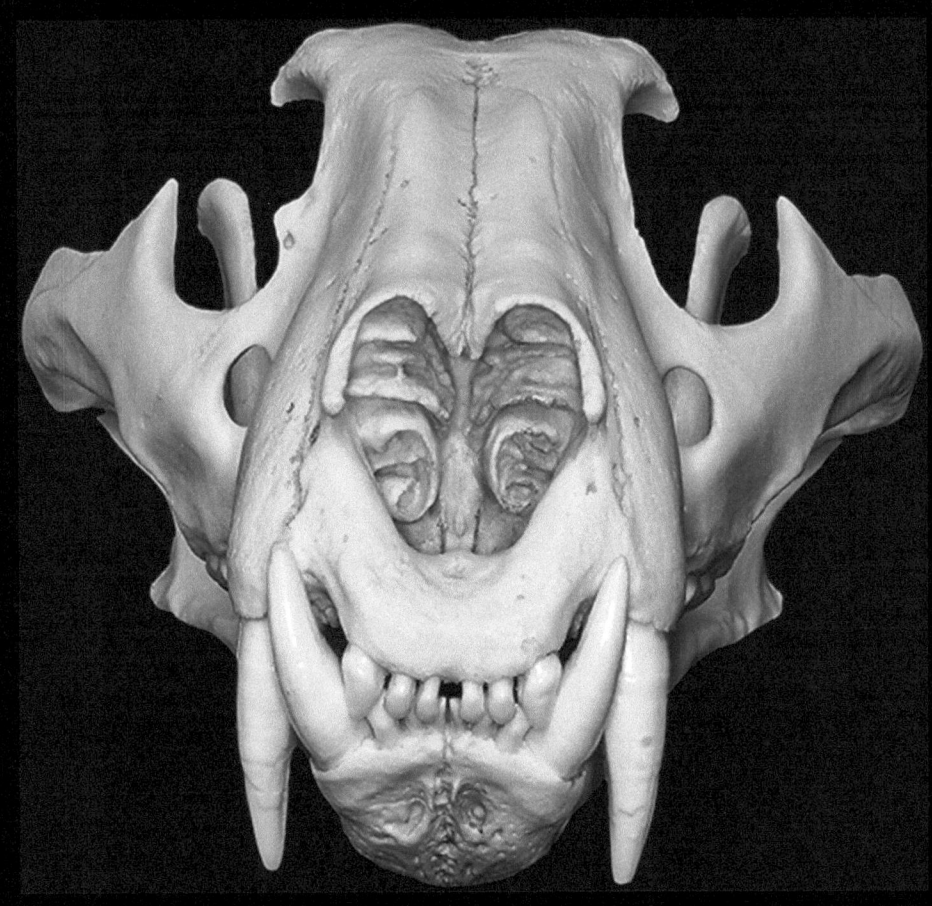

# Water Monitor

Scientific name: *Varanus salvator*

Water monitors are one of the most common monitor lizards in the Southern part of Asia. Some people keep them as pets but you probably wouldn't want to do that. They can grow more than 7 feet (2.1 meters) long, they have a vicious bite, sharp claws and a powerful tail which they can use to cause serious damage to peoples' legs, arms and hands. They have also been known to carry a bacteria called **salmonella** which can make people very sick.

In Thailand, the word for water monitor is sometimes used as an insult.

The U.S.S. Monitor was the first ironclad ship commissioned by the Union Navy in the Civil War.

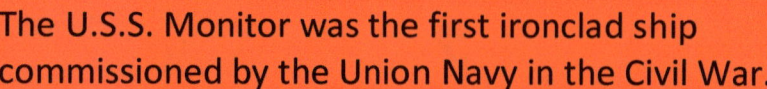

# ZEBRA

Scientific name: *Equus grevyi*

(Grevy's zebra)

The pattern of each zebra's stripes is unique – just like the pattern of your fingerprints is unique to you. You might think that the zebra's black and white stripes would make it easy for predators to see them, but that's not the case. When a herd of zebras squeezes close together, the stripes form a confusing pattern. That makes it difficult for a predator to pick out one specific animal to attack.

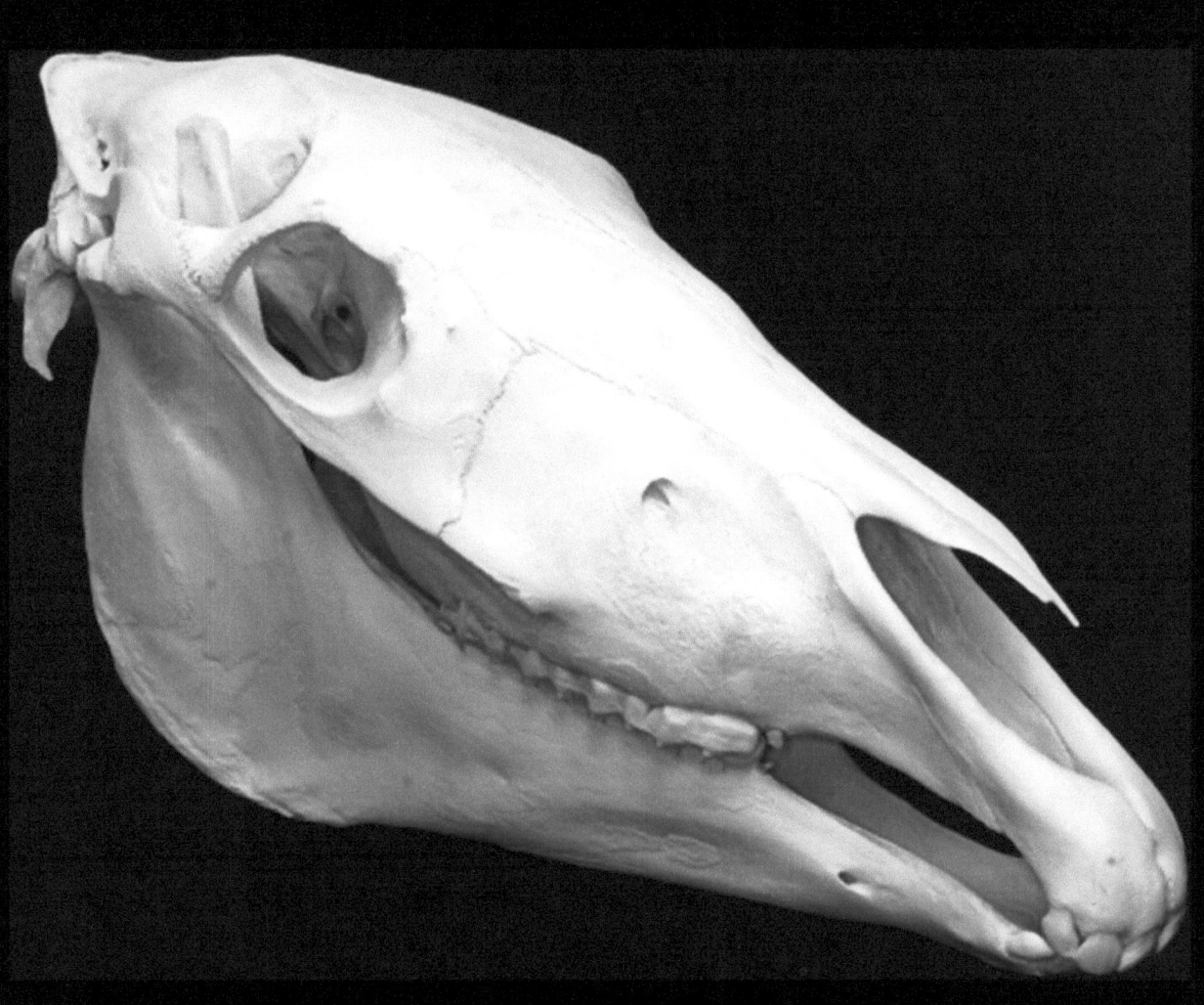

# SKULL MATCH

Can you match the animal with its skull?

(Answers are at the bottom of the first page of this book.)

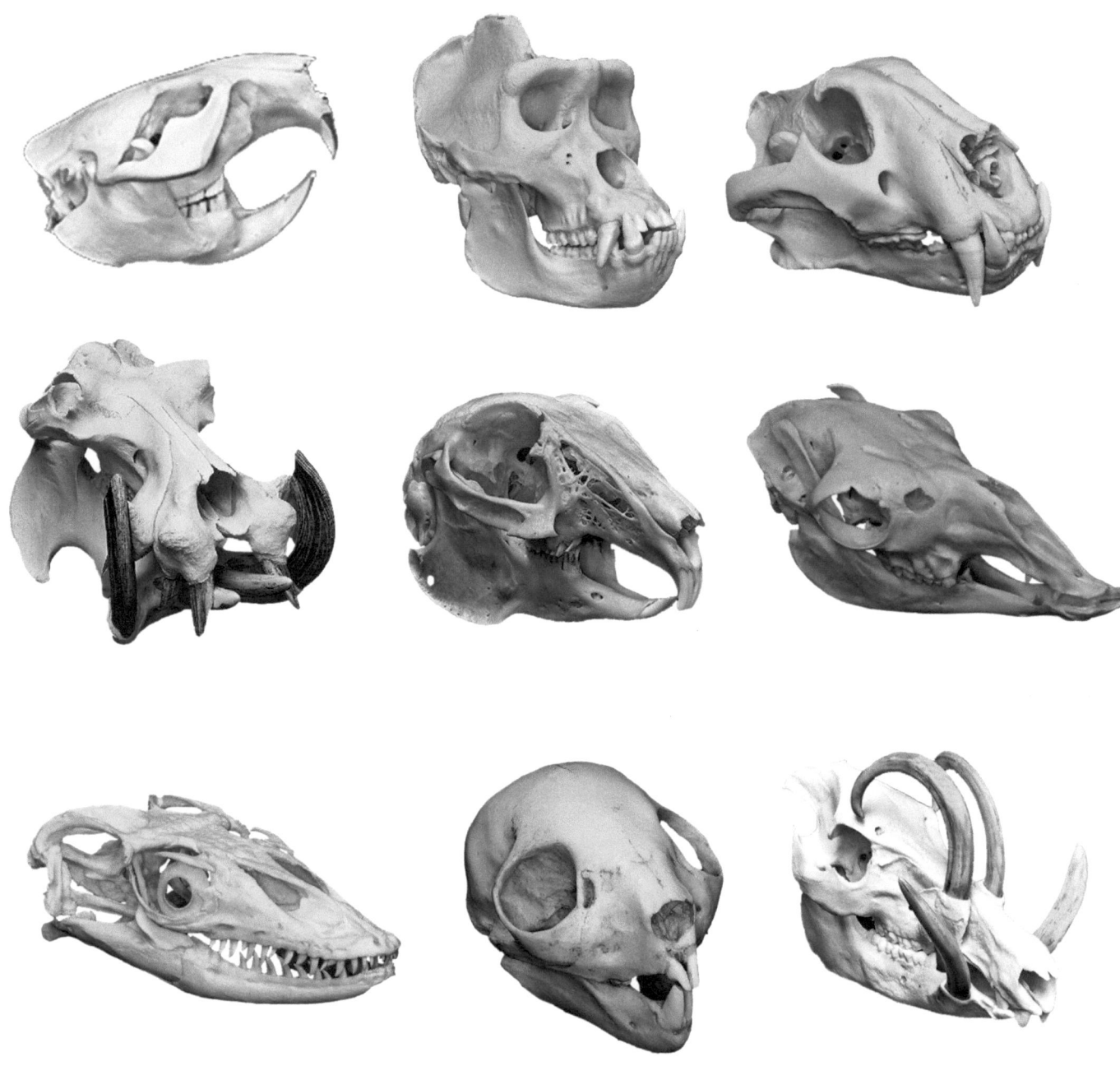

56

Cetaceans – A group of animals that includes whales and porpoises.

Cranium – The part of the skull that covers and protects the brain.

Crepuscular – Active when the sun is coming up (dawn) and when the sun is going down (dusk).

Frugivorous – Frugivorous creatures eat only fruit.

Idiom – Idioms are expressions people use to mean something different than the actual words. An example is: It's raining cats and dogs.

Intestines – The part of the body inside people and some animals that is connected below the stomach. The intestines take the good stuff from food and push the rest out of the body.

Marsupial – Marsupials give birth to babies that are not fully developed. Most marsupials carry their young in a pouch until the babies are fully developed.

Nocturnal – Active at night.

Omnivorous – Omnivorous creatures get their food from plants as well as meat.

Primates – A group of creatures that includes humans, apes, monkeys and lemurs.

Salmonella – A bacteria that can cause food poisoning.

# WANT MORE INFORMATION?

http://www.aqua.org/ - Web site of the National Aquarium in Washington, D.C.

http://www.animalfactguide.com/ - Includes videos of rare animals.

http://switchzoo.com/ - Animal games, puzzles and other fun stuff.

http://www.nwf.org/Kids/Ranger-Rick.aspx - Ranger Rick magazine from the National Wildlife Federation. Includes photo contest, jokes, Q&A.

http://kids.nationalgeographic.com/ - National Geographic's web site for kids. Includes, "Bet you didn't know" section of cool facts.

http://www.kidsbiology.com/ - Kids Biology website with tons of info about animals and plants plus worksheets, coloring sheets, etc.

www.ingramcontent.com/pod-product-compliance
Lightning Source LLC
Chambersburg PA
CBHW041533040426
42446CB00002B/71